Boost Your Child's Fitness

This book is for Ava Violet, who has been keeping me fit and active since the day she was born.

Teach®
Yourself

Boost Your Child's Fitness
Ceri Roberts

For UK order enquiries: please contact Bookpoint Ltd,
130 Milton Park, Abingdon, Oxon OX14 4SB.
Telephone: +44 (0) 1235 827720. Fax: +44 (0) 1235 400454.
Lines are open 09.00–17.00, Monday to Saturday, with a 24-hour
message answering service. Details about our titles and how to
order are available at www.teachyourself.com

Long renowned as the authoritative source for self-guided
learning – with more than 50 million copies sold worldwide –
the **Teach Yourself** series includes over 500 titles in the fields of
languages, crafts, hobbies, business, computing and education.

British Library Cataloguing in Publication Data: a catalogue record
for this title is available from the British Library.

First published in UK 2008 by Hodder Education, part of
Hachette UK, 338 Euston Road, London NW1 3BH.

This edition published 2010.

Previously published as *Teach Yourself Helping Your Child to
Get Fit*

The **Teach Yourself** name is a registered trade mark of
Hodder Headline.

Typeset by MPS Limited, a Macmillan Company.

Printed in Great Britain for Hodder Education, an Hachette UK
Company, 338 Euston Road, London NW1 3BH, by CPI Cox &
Wyman, Reading, Berkshire RG1 8EX.

The publisher has used its best endeavours to ensure that the URLs
for external websites referred to in this book are correct and active
at the time of going to press. However, the publisher and the
author have no responsibility for the websites and can make no
guarantee that a site will remain live or that the content will remain
relevant, decent or appropriate.

Hachette UK's policy is to use papers that are natural, renewable
and recyclable products and made from wood grown in sustainable
forests. The logging and manufacturing processes are expected to
conform to the environmental regulations of the country of origin.

Impression number	10 9 8 7 6 5 4 3 2 1
Year	2014 2013 2012 2011 2010

Acknowledgements

I would like to say a big thank you to my partner, Rob Mansfield, and my mum, Maureen Roberts, for all their help and support while I was writing this book.

Acknowledgements

Contents

Meet the author

As parents, we have never been under quite so much pressure to keep our children active and healthy. Seldom a week goes by without newspaper reports about the dangers of childhood obesity, or news of routine school health checks that label perfectly healthy and active children 'overweight'. Amid all this fuss and confusion, it's hard to know what to do for the best. How do we know if our children are actually overweight? Should we shrug off government warnings and reassure ourselves that they seem happy and healthy enough as they are? After all, don't *all* kids spend half their time watching TV and eating junk food? Or should we lay down the law, ban sugary treats and put extra stress on the whole family as we struggle to implement a healthy eating and exercise regimen? The answer, of course, lies somewhere between these two extremes.

Anyone who has tried – and failed – to get fit or lose weight knows that that it's hard work. But that's usually because we *make* it hard work. After all, if quick-fix diets and celebrity workout DVDs really worked, we wouldn't need to start a new one at least once a year, would we? However, helping your child to get fit is a totally different proposition. No right-thinking parent would encourage their child to drink meal-replacement shakes or eat nothing but cabbage soup. Neither would you encourage them to exercise until they can't catch their breath and feel dizzy. If you want your child to enjoy exercise and eating healthily, then you need to make it enjoyable. Believe it or not, that really is an achievable goal.

Children learn by example, so if you want to make sure that they are eating a healthy diet and enjoying an active lifestyle, you first need to take a long, hard look at yourself. If you maintain a healthy weight, eat plenty of fruit and vegetables and keep sweet treats to a minimum, then it's unlikely that your children will have picked up too many bad habits. But if you rely on takeaway meals, snack on junk food and drive everywhere rather than walk, then you can't be surprised if your kids do the same.

By the same token, if you hated school sports and have spent years struggling with your weight, then there's a good chance that you have passed on the message to your children that sport is boring and hard work, or that takeaway food and chocolate are tastier and more fun than home-cooked meals. I know that I have been guilty of all of this myself; I hated school sports and was always the last to be picked for games. Twenty years later I still dread team sports to the extent that I refuse to play rounders in the park or volleyball on the beach. But I enjoyed dance classes from the age of five – and it's dance, aerobics and Pilates that I rely on to keep me fit as an adult. I also realized that I had to knock my post-pregnancy chocolate muffin habit on the head once my daughter was weaned and started to take an interest in what I was eating. I couldn't very well get away with feeding her banana and carrot sticks when I was eating cakes!

Medical research has proved that lifestyle has a huge impact on our health, so making some effort to eat well and keep fit and active is the best insurance policy for you and your family. That's not to say that you have to be too strict about it; in fact, you'll get the best results if the changes you make are so small that your children barely notice the difference. My daughter prefers home-made potato wedges to chips – and she loves vegetables and olives on her pizza. Most of the time she snacks on apples, bananas and breadsticks rather than crisps, but that doesn't stop us baking – and eating – cookies and fairy cakes. She loves chocolate too, but I buy fun size packs so that I know exactly how much she's eating. She likes cucumber, but won't touch lettuce and tomatoes. She's happy to go out on her scooter, but complains if I try to persuade her to walk to the shops. Rather than making her eat or do something she doesn't enjoy, I've found that it's much better to focus on what she *does* like.

So we take her scooter to the shops, and we cook banana muffins with honey rather than buying sugary, shop-bought cakes. I introduce new things every once in a while, but if she doesn't like something, I don't make a big deal about it and suggest something else instead. This keeps both of our stress levels low, and means she's much more open to new ideas and experiences as a result.

Admittedly, the earlier you start with this, the easier it is, as it's much simpler to build good habits than break bad ones. That said, it only takes a little effort to make lasting changes. So don't get overwhelmed with thoughts of diets and exercise. Instead, focus on your family: what do your kids like to eat? What do they like to do? Don't try to change your family's habits overnight – you are far more likely to succeed with a 'softly, softly' approach. Most importantly: start today, not tomorrow; serve extra vegetables with dinner tonight, and walk to the shops to buy them. Incorporating these small changes into your daily routine really can help your child – and yourself – to get fit, and this book contains all the information you need to get started.

Only got a minute?

Keeping fit and active can help to reduce the risk of developing a range of illnesses, including heart disease and cancer. It can also boost immunity, energy levels and concentration. Experts agree that children are now getting significantly less exercise than previous generations, and this has led to an obesity epidemic as many children now consume more calories than they burn off.

British Medical Association (BMA) guidelines recommend that children should undertake a minimum of 60 minutes' moderate exercise each day. If your child is not used to exercise, then it's wise to aim for 30 minutes initially, and gradually increase this until it becomes part of their everyday routine.

It can be difficult to motivate children to get fit, but it helps to think of ways that you can get fit as a family. Walking, cycling, swimming, ball games, in-line skating and horse riding can all be enjoyed by the whole family, many of them at minimal cost.

Some children might need lots of encouragement to get active, particularly if they are unfit, overweight or don't enjoy school sports. Activities such as dancing, martial arts, skateboarding or water sports might suit them better, or they might prefer a computer dance-mat game or mini trampoline so that they can get fit at home.

Don't overlook the importance of PE as part of your child's school curriculum, as being fit can improve their long-term health and happiness. Some children prefer team sports, while others do better with individual activities.

Eating a healthy, balanced diet will give your child more energy and will help them to maintain a healthy weight. Keep an eye on portion sizes, and limit sugary drinks, junk food and sugary snacks. This will help to keep your child fit for life.

5 Only got five minutes?

There are many reasons why children are now less active than ever before. In part, this is because modern life is so much more convenient – we drive rather than walk, watch more TV (which we operate with a remote control), and we are more likely to connect with friends by phone, text or internet than by meeting up – or playing – face to face.

Many parents are now understandably reluctant to let their children play outdoors, in the way that was normal for us as children. A study by Play England has shown that one in four eight- to ten-year-olds have never played outside without an adult – and if children aren't running around the park or riding their bike, they are probably staying safely at home, sitting on the sofa where their parents can keep an eye on them.

Is my child getting enough exercise?

Doctors recommend that children should be active for a minimum of one hour each day. If your child isn't getting this much exercise at the moment, then aim for 30 minutes of daily activity and build up from there. If your child isn't keen on sports, then you might find it helpful to think of ways that you can change their habits, such as walking to school, taking the stairs, or visiting the playground – this will help them to become more active without feeling that they are being forced to exercise.

Family fitness

The most effective way to help your child to get fit is for the whole family to exercise together. This not only sends a message to your child that being active is a routine part of life, but it also encourages you to spend more quality time together – and can even be fun! Most families find it works best to set aside some regular time at the weekend, perhaps on a Sunday – and you can vary the activity you choose according to the weather and your energy levels.

Making fitness fun

If you and/or your child don't enjoy sports or physical activities, then getting fit can feel like a daunting task. In order to make fitness fun, you need to think carefully about the activities that you and your child enjoy. Some sporty parents try to push their children into playing football or tennis just because they enjoy it. If their child doesn't have a natural ability, they then feel like a disappointment and a failure – which will only serve to prove that they are 'not sporty'.

Activities that are not considered to be particularly sporty – especially those that aren't a part of PE lessons – are more likely to appeal to children who aren't particularly active. You could try dancing, dressing up and active role play, skateboarding, go-karting, water sports, horse riding, dog walking, indoor play centres, martial arts or trampolining.

School sports

Some parents overlook their child's performance in PE because they assume that it's not as important as their academic work. However, children's participation in – and enjoyment of – PE lessons, can have a great impact on their long-term health and happiness. It can also help them to build and develop important skills such as team building, problem solving, leadership and coordination.

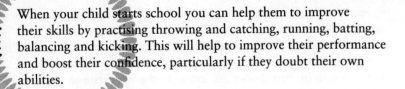

When your child starts school you can help them to improve their skills by practising throwing and catching, running, batting, balancing and kicking. This will help to improve their performance and boost their confidence, particularly if they doubt their own abilities.

Nutrition

Children's nutritional requirements vary with age, weight and activity levels – so it can be difficult to work out what, and how much, they need to eat. As a general rule, it's wise to avoid processed junk food, and eat as much fresh produce as possible. That means snacking on fruit instead of chocolate and crisps and serving vegetables or salad with meals.

Remember that young children don't need to eat as much as adults, so you will need to adjust their portions accordingly. Aim for around two-thirds the size of an adult portion for children under ten; by the time children reach their teens they will usually need to consume more calories than their parents. Provided that your child is eating healthily most of the time, the occasional treat won't be a problem.

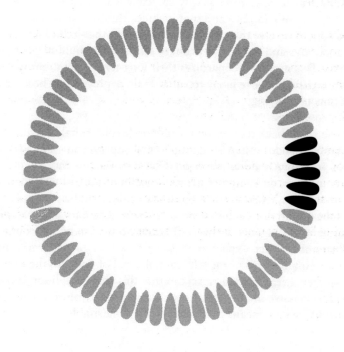

10 Only got ten minutes?

Most young children are naturally energetic and blessed with the boundless energy that leaves most parents exhausted. So why do we need to worry about helping them to get fit?

Media reports about the obesity epidemic warn that we are all getting steadily fatter – and that includes children. If we don't act now to reverse this trend, experts predict that half of primary school boys and one in five primary school girls could be obese by 2050. This not only jeopardizes their long-term health, but it also means they are more likely to suffer from depression or become victims of bullying.

If you think back to your own childhood, you probably remember playing outside – often without parental supervision – in a way that your own children never do. Children are now more likely to play indoors, on computer games consoles or the internet, than they are to ride bikes or run around outside with their friends. Adults are no different – we have far more sedentary lifestyles than our parents did when we were children, so we can hardly complain when our children expect to be driven to school or prefer to slump on the sofa in front of the television instead of going to the park with their friends. Scientists claim that this change in lifestyle has lead to 'passive obesity': we now consume more calories than we burn off, which means that weight gain is inevitable.

Realistic changes

British Medical Association guidelines recommend that children should be active for a minimum of one hour each day. This might sound a lot, but it doesn't have to be done in all one go. Also, strict diet and exercise plans seldom work for adults, let alone children – so you need to be realistic about your goals and expectations.

Before you start making plans to join sports clubs and classes, it's best to take a good look at your lifestyle and think about small changes that you can make to your daily routine. For example, if you currently drive your child to school, you could think about walking or cycling – even once or twice each week will make a difference if you don't have the time to do it every day. If mornings are too hectic, you could think about walking home instead. If you don't feel that you have the time, then why not get together with a group of other mums, and set up your own 'walking bus', taking it in turns to walk a small group of children to school every day. This really is one of the biggest – and cost effective – changes that you can make, so it's well worth making the effort.

Children who have active parents are six times more likely to be physically active themselves, so it's down to you to set the tone and show your child that being active is a normal part of life.

Motivating your child

Even if you have been guilty of it in the past, try to avoid labelling your child as 'lazy', 'not sporty' or a 'bookworm' or 'TV addict'. This will only serve to convince them that sports and activities are not for them, and make them less likely to give them a try in case they fail or look stupid.

Research shows that the main reason that children participate in sports and activities is to have fun; kids aren't interested in the health benefits of exercise, so telling them that keeping fit will improve their health is no incentive. Instead, you need to think carefully about what your child enjoys, and find an activity that will tie in with some of their existing interests. Tread carefully, because pushing them into doing an activity that they hate will make them even less inclined to try something else.

If you are competitive, try not to put too much focus on winning, as your child will feel like a failure if they don't measure up.

Keep the focus on building confidence: celebrate every achievement, and offer incentives (such as new trainers, sports equipment or a day out with a friend) to encourage your child to practise and develop their skills.

Keeping fit as a family

Studies have shown that children with fit and active parents are more likely to be fit and active themselves, so it's a good idea to make regular exercise a part of family life. Most of us complain that we don't have enough family time, so set aside a couple of hours every week to enjoy an activity together. Weekends are likely to be the best time, so schedule a weekly swim, a walk or bike ride. You could even learn a new activity together, such as in-line skating, ice-skating, horse riding or golf.

If time is tight, then think about getting a Wii Fit or electronic dance mat. Practice for just 30 minutes each evening and you'll have fun together as you get fit.

School sports

Children who don't do well in PE often develop a negative attitude towards sports and activities that stays with them for life. For this reason, it's important to encourage your child to do their best and devote time and energy to developing and practising the skills that will help them to succeed.

School PE provision has undergone many changes in recent years, and some schools now offer a choice of at least 15 different activities. This means that your child should be able to find something that they enjoy, that they can participate in for the recommended two hours of school sports per week.

Helping your child with school sports

There are many simple but effective ways that you can help your child to improve their performance and feel more confident about school sports.

- ▶ Encourage your child to run as much as possible – perhaps by racing them to a nearby landmark.
- ▶ Throwing and catching are important skills to master, and many young children need help to get the hang of it. Practise with a soft, light ball that fits easily into your child's hand; start close together and move further apart as their skills improve.
- ▶ Use a small, lightweight bat and bouncy ball to teach your child how to bat. When they have mastered this, challenge them to see how many times they can hit the ball.
- ▶ Most children find it easy to kick a ball, but you can help them to kick over greater distances and improve their aim by practising with a target. So help them to build a goalpost, or draw one on a wall.
- ▶ Challenge your child to stand on one leg and balance for as long as they can, balance along a low wall or hop on one leg.
- ▶ Encourage your child to practise handstands, cartwheels and forward rolls to improve their flexibility.
- ▶ Play a range of different games with your child – better still, get a group of parents and children together for a regular practice.

Nutrition

You don't need to be a gourmet chef to cook healthy meals for your family – and it doesn't need to be expensive or time-consuming either. Preparing home-cooked meals can actually save you money – and if you batch cook and freeze extra portions, it can save you time too.

Aim for three meals and two snacks each day, making sure that your family enjoys five portions of fruit and vegetables, and a good variety of foods from each of these food groups: protein, carbohydrate and dairy. It's wise to limit the amount of fat in your family's diet, so opt for skimmed or semi-skimmed milk, reduced fat cheese and yoghurt, and lean cuts of meat.

Until they reach their teens, most children need half to two-thirds of an adult-sized portion, depending on their size and activity levels. Limiting processed foods will automatically reduce the amount of salt and 'bad fats' in your child's diet, so consider replacing takeaways and ready meals with home-made versions. Home-made burgers, pizza, breaded chicken strips and oven-baked potato wedges are just as good – usually much tastier – than the supermarket versions, and are a healthier way to cater for fussy eaters.

Eat together as a family as often as you can, as this will help your child to develop good habits, encourage them to try new foods and stop them from overeating or eating too fast. Just making these small changes can make a real difference to your child's health and weight – so don't wait for tomorrow, start today!

Introduction

If you are reading this book there is a good chance that you are worried that your child isn't getting enough exercise and you have decided that it's time to do something about it. So congratulations for taking the first step towards improving your family's health and fitness!

As a parent, you want to give your child the best start in life and the good news is that it's never too early – or too late – to make positive changes. In fact, there has never been a better time to focus on physical activity, as alarming reports about the increase in childhood obesity will hopefully provide all the motivation you need.

Research from the International Obesity Taskforce reveals that, in the UK, childhood obesity has tripled since 1995. Worryingly, this trend looks set to continue. The government-commissioned Foresight Report predicts that, unless we act now, half of primary school boys and one in five primary school girls could be obese by 2050. This has very serious consequences, as overweight and obese children are at increased risk of a range of serious health issues including diabetes, heart disease and cancer and are also more likely to suffer from depression, low self-esteem or become victims of bullying.

It's tempting to dismiss these reports as scaremongering, but the dangers are very real and experts agree that it's important to make changes now to avoid a potential health crisis. However, it's not all doom and gloom as fortunately there are lots of things you can do to protect your child's health.

Obviously, ensuring that children eat a healthy, balanced diet goes some way to addressing the problem. However, doctors and scientists agree that what children really need is more exercise.

As a society we have become increasingly sedentary and, for most of us, taking exercise is no longer a part of day-to-day life. Where previous generations of children were expected to walk to and from school, play outside every day or take part in organized sports, it has become the norm for children to be driven to the school gates and spend most of their free time playing computer games or watching TV. As a result, children are routinely consuming more calories than they are burning off through exercise – and gaining weight as a result.

Unsurprisingly, experts agree that it falls to parents to set a good example, but we all know that this is often easier said than done. As our working hours increase and our precious leisure time shrinks, most of us find it hard to make the extra time to walk our children to school, walk to the shops rather than taking the car, or visit the local leisure centre for a swim.

Of course, it's even harder to motivate our children if we don't take enough exercise ourselves. For this reason it's helpful to commit to change your habits as a family because it's unfair to expect your child to eat healthily and stay active when they see you snacking on junk food, lounging on the sofa and taking little or no exercise!

Studies have shown that the habits children pick up in their early years will determine their behaviour for the rest of their lives – so if they are overweight and inactive throughout their childhood they are likely to stay that way. But even if your child is within the normal weight range, it's still important to make sure they stay active.

If you need any more incentive, research has shown that regular exercise can aid restful sleep, boost concentration and improve energy levels – benefits that the whole family can enjoy!

Although it's relatively easy to convince parents that their children need to take regular exercise, it's quite a different matter to persuade a child to turn off the TV and get active. However, this book isn't about making your child follow a punishing exercise regime or pushing them outdoors to exercise whatever the weather. All children are different and there really is no one-size-fits-all approach to fitness.

If you really want to help your child get fit it's vital to identify an activity that your child enjoys. After all, we all know that if exercise feels like a chore, it's impossible to commit to long-term changes. Sooner or later those good intentions will fall by the wayside and you will easily slip back into bad habits. Instead, this book will help you implement gradual changes, so that keeping fit and active simply becomes a way of life.

In the following chapters you will learn why it's important for your child to be active and how to determine the amount of exercise they need. You will also find helpful tips and suggestions on how to increase your child's activity levels gradually, along with suggestions for fun family activities and outings.

Parents of young children will learn how to take advantage of their toddler's boundless energy, along with suggestions for fun games and activities for children who are either too young to take part in organized sports or are not interested in typically 'sporty' pursuits.

From Chapter 6 onwards you will find information on school sports and how to boost your child's confidence and improve their skills. You will then find information on both team sports and individual activities, along with guidelines for finding suitable clubs or coaching facilities and advice on how best to support and encourage your child.

Parents who have specific concerns about a range of practical issues including bullying, competitiveness and safety will find useful help and advice in Chapter 9, alongside information for parents whose children suffer from asthma or have disabilities.

The final chapters of the book are aimed at parents who are worried that their child is overweight or not eating a balanced diet. Here you will find advice on nutrition that will not only help with weight management, but also identify the foods your child should be eating for optimum energy.

Once you have read the first two or three chapters, this book is designed so that you can dip in and out and easily find the information that is most relevant to your child's situation and needs. You will find plenty of straightforward, practical advice that will help you to make the right decisions for your child, regardless of your own experience of, or interest in, a range of sports and activities.

If you are worried that you don't know what your child should be doing, how long they should be doing it for, or are struggling to overcome your child's resistance to exercise, then you will find plenty of real-life case studies, some of which are certain to be relevant to your own circumstances. These should give you some idea of how to overcome the most common problems that you may be facing and will hopefully prove to you that it's worth the effort to continue!

Making any kind of change can be daunting, and it would be unrealistic to assume that it will be plain sailing. But making the decision to get your family active will not only benefit your health but will also increase the amount of quality time you spend together – and will give you much more energy to cope with the stresses and strains of your busy lifestyle.

Remember, even simple lifestyle changes such as walking to the shops can make a difference. Every little helps, so make some small changes today and set the foundations for a healthy and active future.

If your family is new to exercise or you have any health concerns, it's advisable to check with your GP before you begin a fitness programme or healthy eating regime. Bear in mind that the medical advice offered in this book is a guideline only, and is no substitute for proper medical advice or supervision.

1

Getting fit

In this chapter you will learn:
- *why it's important for your child to maintain a healthy weight*
- *why it's important to be fit and active*
- *how much exercise your child needs.*

Why it's important to be active

As adults, we tend to associate fitness with a demanding new regime, fashionable fads made popular by celebrities, and expensive hobbies such as skiing. The rewards, as we see them, are often unrealistic – we aim for fast weight-loss, and the sort of defined muscle tone that means we'll look great on the beach. More often than not, our plans to 'get fit' begin in January and are forgotten by February, by which time we've become fed up and disillusioned because there's still no sign of that elusive six-pack.

So if you're going to make the effort to motivate your child – and your family as a whole – to become more active, then it's important to start with a fresh approach that you can maintain long term. Yes, keeping fit should have a noticeable effect upon the way you look, but there are many more valuable benefits for the entire family that could significantly improve both the quality and the length of your lives.

Keeping fit and active can:

- *help to prevent or control diabetes*
- *reduce the risk of developing heart disease*
- *reduce the risk of cancer*
- *increase energy levels*
- *promote restful sleep*
- *boost the immune system*
- *increase self-confidence*
- *relieve depression*
- *help to maintain a healthy weight*
- *improve bone density and protect against osteoporosis*
- *improve concentration*
- *reduce stress.*

If you are not convinced that you can find the time or energy to take more exercise, then consider how the benefits listed above could transform your day-to-day life. Regular exercise will boost your immune system so that you and your family will be less susceptible to common ailments such as colds, flu and tummy bugs. Your child will be more likely to sleep well at night – which means that you stand a better chance of having an undisturbed night, too – and you'll also have more energy to get through a busy day. If you often feel stressed, or you suffer from depression, exercise can help you to relax and enjoy an increased sense of wellbeing – and your child is more likely to be happy and contented too. If a magic pill that could achieve all this appeared on the market, parents would be queuing up to buy it – regardless of the price. But by making a commitment to get your family fit, you could soon be enjoying all these benefits free of charge.

Insight
If you can't face the thought of exercise, then resolve to do something for just five minutes. When five minutes is up, you will probably decide you can keep going for a little longer. If not, then stop and try again later. A few five- or ten-minute sessions quickly add up.

What is fitness?

We all talk about 'getting fit' but many of us have no idea what
this actually means, aside from a vague notion that it will help
us to look and feel better. From a scientific perspective, the only
way to become physically fit is to take part in regular activity that
causes your body to burn more calories than if you were sitting
still. Of course, this could include anything from climbing the stairs
to running a marathon. That's why experts talk about two types
of fitness: health-related and performance-related. We have already
discussed the benefits of health-related fitness: it protects the heart,
strengthens muscles and bones and creates a sense of wellbeing –
all benefits that are difficult for us to see or measure.

Insight
Getting fit doesn't mean that you should exercise so hard that
you feel uncomfortable or breathless. Regular activity is the key,
and daily walks are a great way to build your child's fitness.

The benefits of performance-related fitness are speed, balance,
agility and coordination, all of which can be identified and
measured through participation in organized sports. In this case,
fitness can be measured in terms of performance – as children
become faster, stronger or more skilled at their favourite sports,
their overall fitness will improve too.

THE BASIC ELEMENTS

When measuring fitness, experts tend to focus on three crucial
elements: strength, endurance and flexibility. Despite what you

might think, strength isn't just about weight training or bulging biceps. In fact, lifting weights isn't recommended for children as it can put their developing bones and muscles under too much stress. Instead, weight-bearing exercise such as climbing, skipping or jumping is the best way for children to build their strength.

Endurance is developed through aerobic exercise – the type that increases the heart rate and speeds up breathing. This protects the heart and lungs and improves the body's ability to circulate oxygen. Children can improve their endurance through activities such as running or jumping.

Flexibility refers to the ease with which muscles and joints can stretch and bend, without stiffness or discomfort. Young children tend to be naturally flexible, but bending, stretching, dance and gymnastics will help them to stay that way.

Ideally your child should take part in a range of activities that will help to build strength, endurance and flexibility – but something as simple as a trip to the playground can cover all three aspects, so there's no need to focus on performance or competition if your child finds that intimidating or off-putting.

Insight

If you keep the focus firmly on fun, there's every chance that your child won't suspect that you're on a mission to get them fit – and there's no need to tell them. Focus on activities that your child enjoys and sell it to them as a treat. This is the most effective way to make exercise a routine part of their life.

The obesity epidemic

Obesity has become such a serious problem that the World Health Organization has described it as a 'global epidemic'. Countless studies show that childhood obesity is at an all-time high – and continues to rise. The National Heart Forum research predicts that 24 per cent of boys and 38 per cent of girls aged 2 to 17 will be overweight or obese by 2020, and leading experts from the National Obesity Forum predict that this generation of children will be the first to have a shorter life expectancy than their parents due to weight-related illness.

Think back to your own schoolmates and you can probably only remember one or two overweight children. Wait outside the school gates for your own child and you will see the evidence of the obesity crisis before your eyes: there are more overweight children than ever before. Worryingly, we are already living with the consequences as doctors are reporting that weight-related problems are on the increase in children. Type 2 diabetes, a disease usually found in middle-aged, overweight adults, is now being diagnosed in children, and obesity is the most important risk factor associated with the condition. Doctors warn that the onset of diabetes in childhood heightens the risk of associated complications, including cardiovascular disease, kidney failure, eye problems and limb amputations, by early adulthood.

Being overweight or obese also means that your child is at risk of developing joint problems, arthritis, digestive problems and hormonal imbalances. It usually leads to weight problems in later life too. This is because fat cells are laid down during childhood. If fat is stored quickly, then the body responds by creating additional fat cells. Consequently, an obese child can have as many as three times the number of fat cells as a child who is a healthy weight. By the time a child reaches adulthood, new fat cells can no longer be created, but they can shrink or swell to accommodate more or less fat. As a result, those who were overweight during childhood often struggle to lose weight as adults because their bodies have more fat cells, so they have a natural predisposition to store extra fat.

Along with the physical problems associated with obesity, overweight children are more likely to suffer from low-self esteem and depression, and become victims of bullying. The school playground can be a cruel place, and name-calling and spiteful comments can make a child's life thoroughly miserable. Studies suggest that girls are more likely to suffer in this way than boys, and the effects of bullying can have a profound and long-lasting effect on a child's confidence.

> ## Insight
> Tread carefully if your child is already conscious of their weight. Don't talk about diets, but focus on healthy eating and exercise for the whole family so that your child doesn't feel that they have been singled out.

The shocking statistics

▶ *The World Health Organization claims that over 1 billion people worldwide are overweight, and at least 300 million are obese.*

▶ *The UK population has grown steadily fatter: 23 per cent of the population is now obese – three times as many as in 1980.*

▶ *According to the International Obesity Taskforce, worldwide more than 22 million children under the age of five are severely overweight, as are 155 million school-age children.*

▶ *According to US Centers for Disease Control and Prevention data, about 15 per cent of US children and adolescents are obese.*

▶ *The BMA Childhood Obesity Report (2005) revealed that in the UK, approximately 1 million children under the age of 16 are obese.*

▶ *New research from the Johns Hopkins Bloomberg School of Public Health, the Agency for Healthcare Research and Quality, and the University of Pennsylvania School of Medicine, predicts that 86 per cent of US adults will be overweight or obese by 2030.*

▶ *Research from London Metropolitan University has shown that British schoolchildren are typically one stone (6.35 kg) heavier than they were in 1977 – and the typical waist measurement has increased by 8–10 cm.*

▶ *Research from the Institute of Child Health at University College London and the Institute of Education, University of London has revealed that almost one-quarter of three-year-olds living in the UK are overweight or obese.*

> ▶ *In the US, 10 per cent of two- to five-year-olds, and 15 per cent of children between the ages of 6 and 19 are already overweight. And one in three children is heavy enough to be considered at risk of developing a weight-related problem.*

PASSIVE OBESITY

The main reason our children are getting fatter, say the experts, is down to a concept called 'passive obesity'. To put it simply, this means that as a society we are no longer active enough to burn off the calories we consume – even if we are eating a healthy, balanced diet. Scientists who worked on the Foresight Report explain that 'passive obesity' means it's difficult to avoid gaining weight because the modern lifestyle has made us so much less active on a day-to-day level.

Take a minute to think back to your own childhood. Most parents can remember enjoying a significantly more fit and active childhood than is typical today. Where it was once common for children to walk to school, concerns about 'stranger danger' or road safety mean that most parents understandably prefer to drive children to the school gates. And while most parents have nostalgic memories of the summer days of their childhood spent playing outside with friends, studies show that our own children are unlikely to have the same experience.

Parents tend to assume that their children get enough exercise at school to counteract the time they spending sitting on the sofa at home, but many children receive less than two hours of PE or school sport each week. Although boys are more likely than girls to take part in sport outside school, some children seldom participate at all. For this reason, it's vital to make sure that your child is active at home too.

Insight
Encourage your child to spend some time outside every day, as this will almost certainly increase the amount of exercise they get. Walking to the shop, washing the car or tidying the garden will all help your child to be more active.

How much exercise?

British Medical Association (BMA) guidelines recommend
that children and young people should undertake a minimum of
60 minutes of moderate physical activity each day. One hour of
activity each day might sound a lot to fit into your child's
routine – but it doesn't have to be done all in one go. It can be
broken down into 10- or 15-minute chunks, and can include
activities such as brisk walking, cycling, active play and dance,
along with most sports. It's also recommended to include activities
that build muscular strength, flexibility and bone strength at least
twice a week. This includes activities such as climbing, jumping,
skipping or gymnastics.

If your child is not taking much exercise at the moment, then
aim to build up to this gradually. Initially aim for 30 minutes a
day – perhaps a walk to or from school, a bike ride, or trip to the
playground after school. The most important thing is to gradually
increase your child's daily activities, so that over time keeping fit
becomes an accepted part of their daily routine.

QUIZ: DOES YOUR CHILD NEED MORE EXERCISE?

This simple quiz will help you to establish if your child needs to be more active.

Does your child walk to school?	Yes/No
Does your child watch more than two hours of television each day?	Yes/No
Do you regularly go swimming, walking or cycling as a family?	Yes/No
Does your child take part in any regular sports or activities?	Yes/No
Does your child often play outside?	Yes/No

Score two points for every 'yes' answer and one point for every 'no' answer.

If you score 8 points or more:

Your child is probably getting enough exercise to meet the recommended guidelines. Encourage them to stay fit and active, and bear in mind that it can be more challenging to maintain their interest in sport and fitness as they get older.

If you score 5–7 points:

You understand the importance of keeping your child fit and healthy and are well on the way to meeting the recommended guidelines. If you find it hard to motivate your child, consider introducing new activities to boost their enthusiasm.

If you score 4 points or less:

It's unlikely that your child is meeting the recommended guidelines, and in time this will affect their health, weight and wellbeing. If your child is resistant to exercise, begin by thinking of small ways in which you can become more active as a family.

Did you know?

Experts agree that participating in sports can be of great benefit to your child's personal and social development. Training and practising teaches them about motivation, commitment, discipline, respect, responsibility and how to follow directions and rules. They also learn about teamwork, leadership and taking turns – all vital skills, which will serve them well throughout life.

10 THINGS TO REMEMBER

1 *Being overweight puts your child at risk of a range of health problems, and overweight children are more likely to become victims of bullying.*

2 *Experts say that our children are becoming obese as a result of 'passive obesity'. This means that they are not active enough to burn off all the calories they consume.*

3 *Helping your child to get fit can benefit their lives in many different ways. Regular exercise will boost their energy, improve their concentration and help them to sleep better.*

4 *The only way to become fit is to take part in regular activity that causes your body to burn more calories than if you were standing still.*

5 *Your child should take part in a range of activities that help them to build strength, endurance and flexibility. A trip to the playground can cover all three aspects.*

6 *BMA guidelines recommend that children should undertake a minimum of 60 minutes of moderate activity every day. This does not have to be done all in one go but can be broken up into chunks.*

7 *If your child is not used to taking exercise, aim for 30 minutes of exercise each day, and increase this over time.*

8 *Don't assume that your child is getting all the exercise they need at school – many children receive less than two hours of PE each week.*

9 *Running, jumping, dance, gymnastics and playground games such as climbing and swinging are all good exercise for children.*

10 *Participating in sports teaches your child about motivation, commitment, discipline, respect, responsibility and how to follow rules.*

2

Making changes

In this chapter you will learn:
- *how to motive your child to get fit and active*
- *how to find sports and activities that your child will enjoy*
- *how to overcome the most common obstacles to getting fit.*

It's one thing to know that your child needs more exercise, but quite another to convince them that they need to change their habits. What's more, you are probably all too aware that you will need to get active yourself, and this can be a very daunting prospect.

If you are to motivate your child successfully, then you need to set a good example. And if you have a history of failed fitness plans, unused gym memberships and so many exercise machines gathering dust in your spare room that you could furnish your own gym, this probably seems like a tough challenge in itself.

One of the main reasons that we, as adults, fail to meet our fitness goals is because we set ourselves challenges that are totally out of step with the pressures and demands of our lives. So planning to get up at the crack of dawn to exercise, or deciding to walk to work may seem like good ideas in theory, but are often incompatible with busy mornings when you have to get the children to school and get to work yourself. Likewise, walking your child to school is often presented as an easy way to get fit and active, but it's often not achievable for parents with children at different schools, or who live too far away for it to even be an option.

Even if you do live close enough to give it a try, it's much more tempting to jump in the car than risk being late by making painfully slow progress with a dawdling child, getting soaking wet on a rainy day or dealing with the inevitable complaints if your child is used to being driven. But if you want to make a difference to your family's fitness, then it's important to start somewhere, even if you only feel able to make small changes some of the time.

Insight

If you live too far away from school to walk, then consider driving part of the way and walking the rest. This means that your child will still get some exercise, and you'll find it easier to park!

Did you know?

Research carried out by Cannons Health Clubs discovered that 47 per cent of parents are too exhausted to play actively with their children. Interestingly, the study found that of the least active parents, 72 per cent found their children's behaviour irritating. In comparison, 65 per cent of parents who spend one hour or more each day exercising with their children said that they did not find their children's behaviour irritating. So it seems that getting active can make parenting easier!

Getting started

Begin by writing a list of manageable ways in which you could boost your own activity levels in the next week or two. It's fine to start small – the important thing is to set realistic and measurable goals that you are confident you can achieve. Your list might read something like this:

▶ *I will take the stairs or walk up the escalator rather than using the lift.*
▶ *If I take the lift or escalator up, I will take the stairs back down.*

- *I will go out for a walk every day – even if it's just a five-minute walk to the shops.*
- *When I have time, I will walk rather than drive.*
- *When I take the car, I will choose a parking space at the far end of the car park so that I have to walk a bit further.*
- *I will walk faster than usual.*
- *I will watch 30 minutes less television each day and use that extra time to get off the sofa and do something active – housework, mowing the lawn or turning on the radio and dancing around are all options.*

None of these things should take too much time out of your day, and with practice they will become second nature. Not only that, but these goals will also seem more achievable than aiming to visit the gym three times a week, or going jogging every morning. And you probably know from experience that if you fail to meet your fitness goals, it's tempting to abandon them altogether.

After a couple of weeks, sit down with your list and review your progress. You will probably have already discovered that even these small changes will have started to benefit your family as a whole. It's likely that you will all be walking more if you are making the decision to leave the car at home some of the time, but what's really important is that your child will notice that you are being more active and will begin to see this as 'normal'. You will then be in a great position to build on these goals and motivate your child to get fit too.

Insight

Remember that all of these tips are a great way to get started – but you'll need to build on them in order to get your child fit. Use these suggestions as a starting point to help you think about other activities that your child might enjoy.

Did you know?

Children who have active parents are six times more likely to be physically active themselves.

Motivating your child

We are all individual, so it would be foolish to assume that we should all enjoy the same activities. But just because your child seems to prefer playing computer games to running around a football field, that's really no excuse to decide that they are 'not the sporty type' and use that as an reason to make little or no effort to help them to get fit. Even if you have been guilty of it in the past, make an effort to avoid labelling your child as a 'bookworm', 'TV addict' or, worse still, 'lazy'. These labels serve to convince your child that sports and activities are not for them, so they are less inclined to get involved in case they fail or make themselves look stupid.

Insight

If you don't take regular exercise, then take a few minutes to think about the labels that you apply to yourself. If you describe yourself as 'lazy' or 'not sporty', then try to adjust your thinking and find an activity that you can enjoy. If your child sees that you can enjoy keeping fit, they are more likely to understand that it can be fun.

It's important to bear in mind that the reasons why children choose to take part in sports and physical activities are somewhat different to the reasons why adults participate. For example, your child is unlikely to be interested in the health-related benefits of exercise.

To a child, anyone over 20 is ancient, so telling them that keeping fit will protect their health as they get older is unlikely to motivate them.

Studies have shown that the main reason children participate in sports is to have fun. Other reasons are to do something they are good at, improve their skills, be with their friends and make new ones. Common reasons not to participate include not having enough fun, being under too much pressure and fear of failure or looking stupid. Unsurprisingly, children who don't have much confidence in their own sporting abilities are the least likely to participate. So as a parent, the first step is to find an activity that your child can enjoy, and build their confidence in their ability to do it well.

CHOOSING AN ACTIVITY

Most parents know that finding a sport to suit their child isn't always as easy as it sounds – and it's unlikely that you would have picked up this book if you didn't need a little help getting started. If your child is overweight, unfit, or resistant to the idea of exercise, it's vital to start with a number of small changes. Be aware that putting your child under pressure to take part in a sport or activity they don't like could put them off for life – so tread carefully. At this stage, forget about organized sports and think in terms of adding something to your child's life, rather than taking something away. It might help to think of activities that their friends can get involved in too, or situations where they are able to mix with other children. Perhaps you could suggest taking a friend's dog for a walk in the park, plan a visit to the local pool, a picnic, a trip to the beach or a day out at a fun park, wildlife park or zoo.

Although some of the above suggestions might not seem like particularly active options, your child is much more likely to get moving than if they are sitting in front of the TV all day. Initially, work on the basis of organizing one outing of this kind each week, probably at the weekend. If you're short on time, then suggest meeting friends for a trip to the park, or go bowling. If you have more time, plan a whole day out and check local newspapers or websites for events or attractions that might appeal to your child. Visiting farms, water parks, playgrounds and, for younger children, ball parks and soft play areas can really help you to show your child that being active can be fun.

> ## Insight
>
> Think about ways to treat your child that will also help them to get fit. Instead of rewarding them with a DVD, pizza or computer game, think about a camping trip, day at a fun park or visit to the zoo instead.

INCREASING PARTICIPATION

The next step is to increase your child's activity levels gradually, on a daily basis. Go back to your list, and think of small ways in which you can tweak their routine.

This time, your list could look like this:

▶ *From now on, I will walk my child to school once a week. If mornings are too busy, we will walk home from school instead. If school is too far away to do either, I will walk to the shops, the park or to a friend's house.*
▶ *I will draw up a rota of household chores and ask my child to help.*
▶ *I will gradually reduce the amount of television my child watches each day.*
▶ *I will encourage my child to spend some time outdoors every day.*

At this point, it's very possible that you will meet with some resistance, but it's important to persevere. If it helps, offer a reward or incentive to encourage active behaviour. Make sure that this doesn't involve food or extra time in front of the TV or at the computer. Instead, allow your child to stay up 15 minutes later, invite a friend over to spend the night or ask for their help planning a fun – and active – family outing if they stick to the rules for a month. That way you are rewarding their increased activity with more activity!

You might also find it helpful to pay attention to people in the public eye who your child admires or respects. Point out any evidence that they are enjoying a fit and active lifestyle and draw their attention to any other well-known people who seem happy, successful – and fit. Remember, your aim isn't to criticize people who are overweight or unfit, but to encourage your child to form positive associations and a desire to get fit themselves.

If you follow the suggestions above, you should find that your child will become significantly more active, without doing anything that they would recognize as 'exercise'. By incorporating physical activity into their day in these ways you should be able to ensure that even the most resistant child gets around 30 minutes of exercise each day, which means you are already halfway to meeting the recommended government guidelines.

Case study: How to motivate your child to get fit

The problem

Georgie is a nine-year-old girl who is very reluctant to take any exercise. She is an unwilling participant in PE and is self-conscious about her lack of sporting ability. Her parents have tried to boost her confidence by practising running, jumping, throwing and catching but this makes her more self-conscious and often ends in tears. Although she is within the healthy weight range, both her parents are overweight, and concerned that Georgie will gain weight too, unless they can encourage her to become more active.

The solution

Not all children can be natural athletes and some find team games particularly difficult if their lack of sporting ability sets them apart from other, more able, children. Although Georgie's parents were trying to help by practising the basic sporting skills that she is taught in PE, they were inadvertently reminding her of her failings.

So they decided to put a stop the practice sessions, unless Georgie specifically asked for help, and focus on other activities that she might enjoy, or at least not object to.

The outcome

Georgie's parents were keen to start with an activity which doesn't require expensive equipment, so ice-skating seemed like a good option as skates are available to hire at the rink. Georgie was delighted when her parents asked if she would like to go ice-skating with some friends, and her new hobby has been a big success. Georgie and her friends now go to the ice skating 'disco' every week and their respective parents all take turns to drive them there. The girls are now beginning to express an interest in rollerblading, and Georgie has asked for a pair of in-line skates for her birthday. She still doesn't enjoy PE, but Georgie's parents have accepted that she can be active in other ways and are happy that she has found an activity that she enjoys.

Finding the right activity

Although it's important to fit lifestyle activities such as walking and visiting the playground into your child's routine, this isn't really enough to meet the BMA recommendations or to get your child fit. What's more, participating in sports can benefit your child in other ways. Properly structured sports and activities can help your child develop confidence, social and leadership skills, and show them how to set themselves goals and targets and work towards achieving them.

So how do you find an activity that your child might enjoy? Often this comes down to trial and error, but by thinking carefully about your child's hobbies, interests and personality type you can put together a list of sports and activities that they will at least find acceptable, if not immediately appealing.

FITNESS PERSONALITY TYPE

As a starting point, you may find it helpful to work out your child's fitness personality. So read through the following three types and identify the one that most resembles your child:

▶ *The non-athlete: This child is not interested in sports or physical abilities, sometimes because they lack ability, confidence or are overweight.*
▶ *The casual athlete: Most children fall into this category. This child is not a star sports player but is interested in various activities. However, they are likely to lose interest or give up if their performance is criticized or they are put under too much pressure.*
▶ *The athlete: This child enjoys sport and activities and has a natural ability.*

If your child is natural athlete, you are unlikely to be reading this book as they will probably be participating in a range of sports and activities already. If your child is a non-athlete, the first step is to find ways of building confidence and identifying enjoyable activities that they won't find uncomfortable or embarrassing. The casual athlete often thrives on parental support and encouragement, but is likely to worry about the reactions of peers or teammates. For this reason, you might find that they do best in individual activities such as swimming or dance, where they can work at their own pace and focus on their own achievement without worrying about the expectations of their teammates.

SOCIAL PERSONALITY TYPE

Next, think about your child's personality type. If they are sociable and find it easy to make friends, they may be happiest as part of a team. So for older children consider football, netball, basketball and hockey. For children under six years of age, who are generally considered too young to take part in this kind of organized sport, think about activity clubs or playground games where they can mix with other children.

If your child is shy or prefers to do their own thing, they are more likely to enjoy activities that don't force them to spend time with children they don't know or find intimidating. So think about activities you can enjoy together as a family such as bike rides, walking or swimming.

If your child loves being the centre of attention, they may find activities which reward individual performance to be the most enjoyable. Dance classes and gymnastics are ideal, but take care not to put too much pressure on your child to excel as this may put them off altogether.

It also pays to capitalize on your child's interests. Boys who are mad on computer games might respond well to martial arts classes. Animal lovers might enjoy horse riding – and many stables offer free rides to children who help muck out stables and groom the horses, which is a great way of getting fit in itself. Girls who dream of becoming pop stars would probably jump at the chance to take dance classes, while children who prefer reading to running around might respond well to learning a new skill, such as fencing or golf. Children who enjoy arts and crafts might be tempted out for a walk if you promise to help them collect leaves or stones to make a collage, while nature lovers might prefer a nature walk, particularly if you note down all the animals and birds you see on your walk and look them up in a wildlife encyclopaedia when you get home. More detailed information on fun activities, team sports and individual pursuits can be found in Chapters 7 and 8.

Insight

It's far better to work *with* your child than against them. So don't push them to take part in activities that they have no interest in – persevere until you find something that they really enjoy.

Common obstacles to getting fit

No matter how good their intentions, many parents find that it can be a challenge to help their children get fit and active. At one time or another, most parents will encounter one, if not all, of the following obstacles:

- *expense of sports clubs, classes and equipment*
- *lack of facilities in the local area*
- *transport issues*
- *safety concerns*
- *lack of time.*

It's important to remind yourself that all of these obstacles can be overcome in the following ways:

- *Sports clubs and equipment can be expensive, so it's a good idea to borrow or hire the necessary equipment until you can establish if your child is serious about continuing. You could also check if your local council offers any low-cost clubs or classes. Remember that physical activity doesn't have to mean organized sport – if you have access to some outside space, inexpensive items such as skipping ropes, balls, hula hoops and Frisbees can all encourage your child to take part in active play.*
- *If there aren't any suitable clubs or facilities in your area, then look into setting up your own, with the help of your child's school or community organizations.*
- *If transport is a problem, you may find that you can carpool (ridesharing) with other parents or take turns to travel with each other's children on public transport.*
- *If your child is part of an organized club that meets all the recommended safety guidelines, then you shouldn't have too much cause for concern. But if your concerns relate to allowing your child to play outside unsupervised, perhaps you could arrange a rota with other parents where you take it turns to supervise, or perhaps ask older siblings to help supervise instead.*
- *The most pressing obstacle for most parents is time. And this can also be an issue for older children who are coping with increasing amounts of homework. But as we all know, we can usually manage to find time for the things we really enjoy. Really, the only solution here is to make exercise a priority*

and find a way to fit it into your schedule. Cutting back on sedentary activities such as watching TV is often the most obvious solution and if you can find activities that you can enjoy as a family, you may find that you begin to look forward to the time you spend getting fit together. Perhaps you could get together with other like-minded parents and take it in turns to organize regular activities for your children. A weekly game of rounders or football in the park is great way to spend a summer evening, and a fun way for parents to socialize and unwind too.

Case study: Finding the time to exercise

The problem

Amanda is a single working mother with two daughters, Corrine, four, and Emily, seven, who doesn't have the time to get active with her children. She works full time and as one child is at school and the other at pre-school, she doesn't have time to walk them both there in the morning. She feels guilty that she lets her daughters watch television while she gets on with the housework and is worried that the only activities they enjoy together – trips to the cinema or watching DVDs – don't encourage them to be active.

The solution

It's very difficult for parents to find time to get active with their children, and particularly so for single parents or those who don't have friends or extended family living nearby who can help out. In this case, the best solution was for Amanda to find ways to use her time more efficiently, so that she could create a spare hour or two for some family activities. Amanda decided to do her weekly grocery shop online, in order to free up some time on Saturday mornings. She also asked her daughters to help with some of the straightforward household chores throughout the week rather than cleaning the whole house by herself at the weekend. She plays their favourite music as they work so that they can sing and dance along.

(Contd)

As there is a three-year age gap between Corrine and Emily, Amanda found it difficult to come up with activities that they could both enjoy, but a trip to the park with their bikes and scooters usually keeps both girls happy, especially if they can meet friends there. Amanda has found that her daughters are more likely to run around and be active when they are with other children, so she now takes it in turns with other parents to have regular play dates, which means she gets some time to herself, too.

The outcome

Amanda now tries to get out as a family first thing every Saturday morning – even if it's just for a trip to the park. Instead of trips to the cinema, she takes her daughters to the fun park instead, which has designated areas to suit both girls. She has also bought an electronic dance mat for them to play with at home instead of sitting around watching television, and has also bought a trampoline for the garden. Corrine and Emily are much happier now that they get to spend more time with their mum, and Amanda now finds that she rarely has to rely on the television to keep them happy.

Play it safe

If your child is new to exercise, it's particularly important to start slowly and set realistic goals. So whether you're planning a daily walk or more specialized sports training, it's vital to warm up and cool down properly and set the right level of intensity so that your child isn't pushed too hard – or taking it too easy!

For example, if your child has never exercised before, you might decide to introduce a 15-minute walk. As the weeks go on, and your child adjusts to their new regime, you could think about adding one or two minutes each week to ensure that their fitness steadily improves. If your child is overweight, unfit or has any health concerns, then it's advisable to consult your doctor before you begin a new exercise regime.

If your child is keen on horse riding or cycling, then make sure that they wear a correctly fitting helmet. They should always wear a helmet, knee, wrist and elbow pads for skateboarding and rollerblading, and floatation devices are helpful for children who are learning to swim. If your child is taking part in organized sports, their coach or instructor should be able to provide any relevant safety equipment.

Finally, if your child is exercising or playing outside in hot weather they are at risk of heatstroke, sunburn and dehydration. Make sure that your child wears a sun cream with a high sun protection factor (SPF), and re-apply it regularly – and encourage them to wear a hat. In summer, to minimize the risks, try to limit activities at the hottest time of the day (11 a.m. to 3 p.m.) and make sure that your child drinks lots of fluids to prevent dehydration. For more information on safety, turn to Chapter 9.

Now you're ready to get started!

10 THINGS TO REMEMBER

1   *The main reason that children participate in sports is to have fun.*

2   *The most common reasons for not taking part include not having fun, being put under pressure, fear of looking stupid and fear of failure.*

3   *Aim to make small, realistic changes to your child's routine such as taking the stairs or walking to school once or twice each week.*

4   *Avoid labelling your child as 'lazy' or a 'bookworm' as this only convinces them that sports and activities are not for them.*

5   *Think about your child's 'fitness personality' as this will help you to identify activities that are most likely to appeal to them.*

6   *Children under six years are generally considered to be too young to take part in organized sports, so think about activity clubs or playground sports instead.*

7   *Sports equipment can be expensive, so it's best to borrow or hire it until you are sure your child will want to continue.*

8   *If you're short on time, consider getting together with other parents to take it in turns to organize activities and/or transport for your children.*

9   *Make sure that your child wears a correctly fitting helmet if they are going to be cycling, horse riding, skateboarding or rollerblading.*

10 *Always apply sun cream and make sure your child drinks lots of fluids if they are exercising or playing outside in the sun.*

3

Keeping fit as a family

In this chapter you will learn:
- *how to make time to get fit*
- *how to assess your family's fitness*
- *which sports and activities you can enjoy as a family.*

Depending on the age of your children, you will have more or less influence over how they spend their free time. If your children are still very young, then you are likely to find it easier to motivate them to exercise, not least because pre-schoolers usually have plenty of energy to burn off and are naturally active. But by the time your children are approaching their teens, any attempts from you to encourage them to be more active is likely to be met with a withering look and a dismissive shrug, as bad habits will already be well ingrained.

Studies have shown that children with fit and active parents are more likely to be fit and active themselves – so the sooner you can make exercise a part of family life, the better. If you're not already participating in regular exercise yourself, it's likely that you consider it a chore, rather than a pleasure, and you will inevitably communicate this message to your child. But if you can identify fun ways to become more active as a family, you might be surprised to find yourself looking forward to it – and your children will too.

Finding the time

Finding activities that you can enjoy together can have emotional as well as physical benefits. When we are busy with work, school and running a home, family time can be one of the first areas to suffer. Many families no longer manage to sit down and eat together every day, and often spend minimal time together because everyone is juggling so many other demands on their time. Learning and practising a new skill or activity together is a great way to prioritize family time, and gives you an opportunity to communicate with your children in an entirely new way. Families who spend time together and have fun, enjoy more shared experiences and have more to talk about – and this can be a vital way of keeping the lines of communication open as your children grow towards adulthood.

At first, the idea of making time for family activities probably seems very daunting – where will you find the time? For most families, weekends are best, so think about setting aside a morning or afternoon for regular family time. Also consider the times when you are usually all together – maybe early evening, or after school. These are perfect opportunities to fit in short bursts of activity that will steadily help to build fitness – especially during the summer months when it's still light and warm enough to get outside well into evening.

Insight

A good way to get fit as a family is to identify a new activity that you can all learn together. You might find it works best to think of something that your child is likely to be better at than you – such as in-line skating or skateboarding. They will enjoy the fact that they are better at it than you, and you can boost their confidence by asking them for a few tips.

Family fitness

Next, try to think of activities that the whole family could enjoy. If you need some help to set the ball rolling, the following quiz should help to get you started.

QUIZ: FIND ACTIVITIES THAT FIT YOUR FAMILY

Choose the answer that best reflects your family.

1 *Thinking of the family as a whole, how active are you at the moment?*
   a *Not at all – we always drive rather than walk*
   b *Fairly active but we don't participate in any organized activities*
   c *Some members of the family are active, others less so*

2 *Do you enjoy organized sport either as a participant or observer?*
   a *No, not at all*
   b *I can take it or leave it*
   c *Yes, very much so*

3 *How would you describe your own level of fitness?*
   a *Unfit*
   b *Fairly fit*
   c *Fit and active*

4 *Are you currently:*
   a *overweight?*
   b *healthy weight?*
   c *underweight?*

5 *How often can you realistically find the time to get active as a family?*
   a *Less than once a week*
   b *Once a week*
   c *Several times a week*

Mostly As: Up to now, you haven't been active as a family – and that needs to change. Even if you don't enjoy sports, it's possible to find a fun activity that the whole family can enjoy. Get together with friends and organize a trip to your local bowling alley – just make sure you stay away from the burger bar while you're there!

Mostly Bs: Although you have an active lifestyle, you don't regularly participate in organized sports or activities. So think about ways that you can improve your family's fitness and build stamina. Weekend bike rides or swimming sessions are ideal – and don't need to take up too much time.

Mostly Cs: You enjoy sport and exercise, but perhaps you're having trouble encouraging your children to feel the same way. Don't be too competitive or assume that your child will enjoy the same activities as you. Instead, think about a new sport or activity you can learn together. Horse riding, rollerblading or water sports could be the answer.

Learn a new skill together

Over the last few years we tried hard to become more active as a family, but our girls Chloe and Amy made it really difficult. They complained if we made them walk any distance and weren't confident enough cyclists for family bike rides. Then, last summer, I decided that we should all learn how to rollerblade. My husband Nick and I hadn't rollerskated since we were kids, and the girls had never tried it – so we were all complete beginners.

As I suspected, the girls are much better than us – I still fall over all the time – and it's been good for their confidence to be in a position to teach us how to do something. We now go rollerblading every weekend, and the girls love it.

Jane is mum to Amy, ten, and Chloe, eight.

Fun activities for the family

Make the most of your family time by trying out the following activities. Some require a little planning or equipment, but many are easy to fit into a spare half hour and some can even be done at home.

WALKING

Perhaps the safest and easiest way to improve your family's fitness is to take regular walks. Walking 10,000 steps (about five miles) each day has been promoted by the British Heart Foundation as one of the best ways to protect your heart and reduce body fat, lower blood pressure and avoid type 2 diabetes. Older children may need to walk even further (up to 12,000 steps for girls and 15,000 for boys) to get the same benefits, but younger children and those who are overweight or unfit should aim for significantly less.

For best results, gradually increase the number of steps you take each day, based on how active you are right now. The easiest way to measure this is to buy a pedometer. This matchbox-sized gadget costs just a few pounds and clips onto your waistband or belt to measure how many steps you take throughout the day. The average person walks between 3,500 and 5,000 steps each day, so you will probably have to put in some effort to reach the recommended target. Begin by counting how many steps you take on an average day then build up gradually, adding 500 steps to your daily total every week or two, until you reach your target.

Insight

Buying your child a scooter or a doll's pram might make them more willing to walk with you. If your child is younger than four, it might be worth taking a buggy for backup on longer walks.

Although all steps count, it's best to include about 30 minutes of brisk walking each day (this can be done in three ten-minute chunks), which will add up to 2,000–3,000 steps. You may find it easier to encourage your child to walk more if you incorporate it into another activity. So rather than simply 'going for a walk' suggest that you walk to visit friends, to a local attraction, the park, the shops or to school. You could even suggest a treasure hunt or nature walk.

Many primary schools now have a 'walking bus' scheme, where children walk together in a group, with adult leaders. Parent volunteers usually lead the bus, with other children and parents joining along the way. Check with your school to see if they have a walking bus – and if not, you could consider setting one up.

If you have a dog, daily walks are a great way to get fit. If you don't, consider asking a friend or a neighbour if you can walk their dog instead. Running around and playing with a dog makes the prospect of a walk much more enticing for children, so if you've been thinking of getting a dog, this could be a good time to go for it.

Initially keep the walk short and easy, and appropriate to your children's age and ability – so avoid steep hills and uneven tracks and make sure to plan 'escape routes' so that you can cut the walk short if your child gets tired. Go at your child's pace and consider getting together with other families so that your children can walk together.

In addition to daily walks, try to get into the habit of going for a longer walk every weekend. In nice weather, take a picnic and head to a local park or nature reserve and make a day of it. On rainy days, walking around a museum – or even an indoor shopping centre! – is better than sitting in front of the television.

Did you know?
Research has shown that walking to school can improve academic performance and keep your child alert throughout the day – so it's good for the mind as well as the body.

CYCLING

Cycling is one of the best forms of exercise there is – and it's an eco-friendly alternative to using the car for short trips. You can introduce your child to the idea of cycling at a very young age. Most children will enjoy riding a tricycle from the time they are roughly one year old, although they won't be able to steer or pedal at this stage, so buy one with a long handle so that you can push them along.

Sometime between their second and third birthday, most children will be ready for their first bike. If you are considering buying a bike for your child, seek expert advice and make sure you choose a frame that's not too big or too heavy. Many parents attach stabilizers at first, but pedal-free balance bikes are now increasing in popularity. These are suitable for children from 18 months up, and teach them to ride using a walking/gliding motion that helps them to learn to balance.

If your child is learning with a traditional bike, you might find it easier to position the seat on its lowest level so that your child can rest their feet flat on the ground. If you then remove the pedals, they can first learn to balance, then to steer, and finally to pedal, before putting all the skills together. Many parents find this easier than relying on stabilizers, which children often get so used to they find it impossible to balance without them. Most children learn to ride a bike somewhere between the ages of four and nine, with six being about average. However, it's important to let your child go at their own pace, and not push them too hard, as this can take all the fun out of the experience.

Insight

If your child is learning to ride a bike using stabilizers, fix them on the lowest setting and move them higher as your child gets used to the bike. This makes the bike more wobbly, which teaches your child how to balance.

If your child can already ride a bike, a new cycling training scheme called Bikeability teaches children how to cycle safely. The scheme has three levels, beginning with manoeuvring in the playground, through to cycling on quiet roads and finally progressing to busy roads. The first level is aimed at children up to the age of nine, the second at 10- to 11-year-olds and the third is aimed at older children and adults.

Of course, you don't have to wait until your child is able to ride a bike before you can enjoy weekend bike rides together. Babies and toddlers can be strapped into a baby or child seat, from the age of six months up to five years, and baby car seats can be fixed safely into a trailer and used from birth. Remember that it's best to keep journeys short with children of this age, especially with babies under one year who have only just started to sit unsupported.

For older children, you could also consider using a tag-along or trailer-bike. This is a 'half bike', which you can attach to the back of an adult bike, allowing your child to be towed. This gives your child the option of pedalling, or sitting back and enjoying the ride. Tandem bikes – which have two seats – can also be a good option. Child-back tandems are sometimes small enough to be suitable for children as young as six, otherwise you can adapt an adult tandem by fitting 'kiddiebars' to extend the handlebars, fitting a small saddle and using 'kiddie cranks' – a small set of cranks and pedals which can be attached to shorten the length between the seat and the pedals. All of these options can be used to get your child used to family bike rides from an early age, which should make them more confident and enthusiastic about learning to ride by themselves.

Is it safe to cycle?

According to a 2008 study by Cycle England, many parents are stopping their children cycling to school or using their bikes on roads because of growing concerns for their safety. More than half of parents used their bikes when they were school age, but 81 per cent ban their children from doing the same – even though only 3 per cent know someone who has had an accident and the number of cyclists killed or seriously injured on the roads is in long-term decline.

A separate survey for sustainable transport charity, Sustrans, found nearly half of all pupils want to cycle to school, but only 2 per cent of UK school children actually do.

If you need any further reassurance, CTC, the UK's national cyclist's organization, maintains that the health benefits of cycling outweigh the risks by a factor of 20:1. Provided your child's bike is roadworthy, they have been taught to ride safely and are wearing brightly coloured or reflective clothing along with a correctly fitting helmet, the risks should be minimal. Obviously it's still very important to exercise common sense. Young children should always be accompanied, and older children should use quiet roads with low levels of traffic wherever possible.

SWIMMING

Swimming is a great activity for the whole family to enjoy – and the best thing is that all age groups, from babies to grandparents, can join in. Most swimming pools offer structured parent and baby swimming lessons for babies aged three months and over, but some swimming pools recommend that your child should have had their immunizations before they visit the swimming pool, so it's best to check with your GP or health visitor before you begin.

Although swimming is a skill that could save your child's life, it's important to keep the focus on fun and help non-swimmers to relax and enjoy the water. It might have been a popular technique in the past, but pushing your child under or throwing them into the pool is never a good idea, as it is more likely to make them fearful of water than teach them how to swim.

A weekly trip to the swimming pool is the best way to build your child's confidence and teach them to become strong swimmers. Instructors usually recommend starting in shallow water and teaching your child to kick their legs, stretch out their arms and put their faces in the water to get them used to it, plus the movements they will need to make to stay afloat. By the age of four or five, many children are confident enough to begin lessons without their parent in the water with them. By this age, some children have already learned to swim, others will take a while longer, and you may find it helpful to use flotation devices such as armbands, noodles or floats for family visits to the pool. Although building confidence is vital when it comes to teaching your child to swim, over confidence can be dangerous. So you must teach your child that they should never swim alone or unattended – and they should be closely supervised at all times, even after they have learned to swim.

Insight

If you're not a confident swimmer yourself, think about having a few lessons when your child is small. This means you'll be less likely to pass on your own anxieties – such as going underwater, diving or swimming long distances – to your child.

Did you know?

The government has unveiled plans to offer free swimming in council-run pools for children under the age of 16. In a move designed to encourage families to exercise together, the ultimate goal is to provide free swimming for everyone, regardless of age, by the time London hosts the Olympic Games in 2012.

BALL GAMES

Most children learn to kick a ball soon after they start walking, and find basic ball games lots of fun. Toddlers will be happy with a game of catch in the garden or park, and will enjoy learning to kick a ball around. As children get older and are almost ready for school, they will need something more challenging, so if you have enough space, think about introducing games of skittles – look out for fun designs in the shops, some of which may feature your child's favourite cartoon characters. This is also a good time to introduce easy bat and ball games, for example where a soft ball sticks to a bat with Velcro.

School-age children might enjoy the opportunity to practise the games that they learn in their PE lessons. This is particularly helpful if your child isn't confident about their sporting abilities. Taking the time to improve their ability to kick a ball, shoot baskets, catch, throw and hit a ball will improve their skills across a range of sports such as football, netball, rounders, cricket and tennis which they will be introduced to at school.

If you have space, think about fixing a basketball hoop in your garden so your child can get outside and practice. You could also think about buying a Swingball set. Swingball is still one of the most popular children's games and sets can be bought cheaply from most sports shops and department stores. Some of these are suitable from four years up and can be easily packed for trips to the beach and park or used in your garden.

TRAMPOLINING

Trampolines are great fun for children, and a fantastic way to keep them fit and active. Adults tend to enjoy bouncing on them too – and now that garden trampolines have become more affordable, it's a great way to get the family interested in exercise.

Before you get started, there are a few safety considerations to bear in mind. Research published in the journal *Prevention* has shown that trampoline-related broken bones account for over one in ten childhood fractures, and research from the Royal Society for the Prevention of Accidents found that the number of people going to hospital after a trampoline accident has increased by 50 per cent over a five-year period.

Injuries are most likely to occur when more than one person is on the trampoline – and the person who weighs less is five times more likely to be injured. Children under six are particularly vulnerable to injury, so should only use trampolines that are specially designed for their age range.

When you're buying a trampoline, look for one that comes with safety pads and nets to minimize the risk of injury and prevent your child from falling off. It's best to place it on flat, soft ground – so grass, sand or bark is ideal. Make sure that there is 2.5 m clear all the way around the trampoline, so that if your child falls off they won't land on anything that could cause injury, such as toys, garden furniture, steps, hedges or trees. Then, make sure that you set some rules for your children – such as only one person to use it at a time, only bounce in the middle, never go underneath when it's in use and don't use it without adult supervision. Now you're ready to leap into action!

PLAYGROUND GAMES

A trip to the playground is one of the best and most enjoyable forms of exercise for young children, and running around after them keeps you fit too. Climbing, jumping and running around comes naturally in this environment and can easily provide all the exercise your toddler needs.

The best thing about playground games is that you can enjoy them in your own garden too. Basic swing and slide sets can be bought fairly cheaply, but even if you don't have the space, you can introduce your children to some fun playground games that will encourage them to get active. Try classic games such as hopscotch, and don't worry if they are too young to understand the rules – the most important thing is to get them moving. Show your child how to hula hoop, or lie a hoop on the floor and encourage your children to jump inside it. If you have a spare afternoon, create a mini assault-course and invite other families round to join in. This doesn't need to be anything complicated – skipping, climbing over obstacles, balancing, throwing a ball into a bucket or scrambling through a cardboard box or tube tent and doing ten jumping jacks will keep everyone amused for an hour or two. Follow it up with a barbecue and your child won't need any persuasion to do it again and again.

Insight

If there is a playground near your child's school, think about organizing a regular after school meet up with some of your child's friends. This gives them a great opportunity to let off steam and spend some extra time with their friends.

GOLF

Until Tiger Woods came along, golf was a sport most commonly associated with middle-aged men. In actual fact, it's a game that the whole family can enjoy together – and walking around the course is great exercise for everyone.

The rules are fairly straightforward: using various clubs, golfers hit a ball into one of the 18 holes that make up a golf course. Each hole has a guide as to how many times a golfer should need to hit the ball to get it in the hole. This is called 'par'. At the end of the course, golfers compare notes on who played the least number of strokes through the entire game. The golfer who has played the least number of strokes overall, or is closest to or most under par, wins.

If you'd like to introduce your child to golf, take them along to a practice range where they can have a go at hitting balls – and make sure that they are using junior-sized clubs to reduce the risk of injury. Most clubs have designated family days, and even offer classes where the whole family can learn together. Young children might prefer a game of pitch and putt – a shorter version of golf, which doesn't involve so much walking. This can be played on courses around the country, and equipment is usually available for hire, which makes it a much more cost-effective option. Alternatively, you could introduce your child to crazy golf. Crazy golf courses typically include fun obstacles such as windmills, tunnels, dinosaurs and model animals, which make the game more appealing to children. Crazy golf courses are usually found in theme parks, seaside resorts and some playground areas.

ICE-SKATING

Most children love to skate, and although it's increasingly common for open-air rinks to open up in winter, it's also an indoor activity the whole family can enjoy all year round. Most large towns or cities have an ice rink and, as skates are available for hire, you won't have to spend money on specialist equipment before you can give it a go. Regardless of ability, ice-skating is a great aerobic workout, helps to build muscle strength and endurance, improves coordination and balance, and improves posture and flexibility. Family sessions cater for all ages and abilities, and some offer family disco sessions where you can dance to your favourite music. It's best to make sure children wear a helmet when skating, and ensure that you are all wearing lots of layers to keep out the chill and provide some protection from the inevitable falls.

HORSE RIDING

Many children love the idea of horse riding, and it's a great way to get some exercise. Children from the age of three can learn to ride, but the average age for beginners is around six years old. It's advisable to have some professional instruction – usually in small groups – just to cover the basics, and children will usually be taught on a lead rein, with an instructor beside them, until they learn how to start and stop on their own. From there, you can visit your local riding school as a family for a lesson or trek – and could even think about a riding holiday. Most riding schools will provide all equipment, including helmets – all you need is jeans or trousers, boots with a defined heel, and a waterproof jacket in bad weather.

IN-LINE SKATING

In-line skating, or rollerblading as it is sometimes known, gives you a great cardio workout, and also strengthens muscles in the legs, back and shoulders. It's important to make sure that your skates are in good condition, and a helmet, knee and elbow protection should also be worn. For family skating, it's best to stay in the park and learn how to balance, start and stop. Children should never skate on the road.

For safety reasons, avoid skating in wet weather, as slippery surfaces can be dangerous for beginners.

TENPIN BOWLING

Whether you want to compete against each other or play as a team, a trip to your local bowling alley is a great family outing. As it's not an intense form of exercise, you don't have to be particularly fit or strong to be good at, or enjoy, bowling. This means it's a perfect activity for families who aren't used to exercise – and as it's possible to improve your performance quite quickly, it can be a good way to get your family interested in sports and activities. All equipment is available to hire, and many bowling alleys also have amusement areas and pool areas, so there's plenty to keep the kids occupied.

KITE FLYING

Provided you follow a few common-sense guidelines, kite flying is a fun and safe activity for the whole family – and gets everyone outdoors. Flying anything other than a single string kite has been banned in some parts of the UK, so it's advisable to check with your local authority to find out which areas are suitable for kite flying, and if there are any specific regulations, such as maximum flying heights – usually 60 m (200 ft) in the UK.

When flying a kite it's very important to choose a safe location, in a large, open area, free from trees, power lines and train lines. For safety's sake, avoid flying a kite in stormy weather, and if a kite should become entangled in a power line, never attempt to remove it yourself. To be extra safe, build or buy kites made from wood, paper, plastic and natural fabrics, as those made with metallic materials, including aluminium foil, may increase the risk of electrocution should you accidentally get the kite caught in a power line.

It's advisable to fly the kite away from roads, just in case you lose control, and be very careful when running with a kite, in case you stumble or fall. Children should only fly kites with adult supervision – and it's a good idea to wear gloves to protect hands from cuts and scrapes caused by kite lines.

The best weather for kite flying is a cloudy day – looking up into bright sunshine can make it hard to see your kite – with a light wind. Beginners should start with a delta- or diamond-shaped kite, as these can fly in much lighter winds than other types.

Getting active at home

If you don't have the time to get out of the house, then there are lots of ways you can get active as a family without leaving home.

- ▶ *Dancing: Turn your favourite music up loud and dance around the house.*
- ▶ *Wash the car: Stop using the car wash, and get the whole family together to wash the car by hand instead.*
- ▶ *Housework: Set up a rota and get the whole family involved in the housework – cleaning windows, washing floors, vacuuming and dusting are all great ways to get active.*
- ▶ *Gardening: If you have an outdoor space, get the children involved with weeding, raking grass and leaves or growing vegetables or flowers.*
- ▶ *Active computer games: If your children are mad on computer games, consider getting them involved in active games such as Wii Fit or dance-mat games, where you move your feet to mimic steps on the screen.*

TEST YOUR KNOWLEDGE

1 *How many steps does the British Heart Foundation recommend you should walk every day in order to protect your heart, reduce blood pressure and avoid Type 2 diabetes?*

2 *Should children aim for more or less than this number?*

3 *What is a walking bus?*

4 *At what age are most children ready for their first bike?*

5 *What is the average age when children learn to ride a bike?*

6 *From what age can children use baby/child seats on an adult bike?*

7 *At what age are most children ready to begin swimming lessons without a parent in the water with them?*

8 *At what age can children begin horse riding lessons?*

9 *What is the best weather for kite flying?*

10 *Name three ways to get active at home.*

....

Answers

1 *10,000 steps*

2 *Young children should aim for around half, older children may need to walk up to 15,000 steps to get the same benefits.*

3 *It's a scheme where children can walk to school together with adult volunteers.*

4 *Between the ages of two and three*

5 *Six*

6 *Six months*

7 *Four or five*

8 *Three*

9 *Cloudy weather*

10 *Dancing, washing the car, housework, gardening, active computer games*

4

Starting early

In this chapter you will learn:
* *why even small babies need exercise*
* *which activities are best for toddlers*
* *how to keep pre-schoolers fit and active.*

Most parents find that as their children grow older it gets harder to motivate them to take regular exercise. In fact, research shows that most children who give up sports do so as they hit their teenage years when they are easily distracted by other pursuits and parents have significantly less influence on how they spend their spare time.

The best way to combat this, say the experts, is to establish good habits when your child is very young. This way, by the time they reach their teens being active is a routine part of their daily life, so even if they no longer have the necessary time or commitment for organized sports, they will still have an active lifestyle.

Being active from the outset

If you are the parent of a baby, toddler or pre-schooler you might think that it's much too soon to introduce your child to regular exercise – but experts agree that this is the perfect time to do so. Making physical activity a part of your child's life will help them to establish healthy habits that will last a lifetime – so the sooner you can start, the better.

The good news is that it's comparatively easy to make sure that under-fives get the recommended amount of exercise. As any exhausted parent will testify, young children are naturally active. They generally prefer to run rather than walk, can't resist climbing and need little encouragement to spend the afternoon racing around the park. What most adults would call exercise, children of this age would call fun – and they can get all the exercise they need from their favourite pastime: playing.

The benefits of exercise for babies and young children

We all know that children learn about the world around them through play. But you may not realize that regular exercise, games and activities also play a vital role in your child's physical, social and emotional development. Taking regular exercise helps your child to:

- ▶ *build strength*
- ▶ *improve coordination*
- ▶ *improve balance*
- ▶ *develop motor skills*
- ▶ *follow instructions*
- ▶ *get used to being part of a team, class or group*
- ▶ *build social relationships*
- ▶ *get ready for starting school.*

Limiting television time

If your child is under the age of five, it shouldn't be too difficult to limit the amount of time they spend in front of the television, and there are several good reasons for doing so. Although parents tend to assume that children's television is educational, many experts disagree and claim that it does more harm than good. Current

US guidelines maintain that children under the age of two should not watch any television at all, as studies show that it can inhibit speech and language development and may be associated with Attention Deficit Hyperactivity Disorder (ADHD) and aggressive behaviour. There is also a clear link between television viewing and childhood obesity. A recent US study showed that children who watch more than two-and-a-half hours of television each day are not only less active, but also consume more calories, as they tend to snack on unhealthy foods as they watch. So it pays to limit your child's access to the television right from the start, before it becomes a habit that is hard to break.

At this stage, it's more likely to be busy parents who struggle most with reducing the time their child spends watching television – not least because it's tempting to use it as an 'electronic babysitter' to entertain children, freeing-up parents to get on with other things. Unsurprisingly, experts insist that television should never be used in this way. However, most parents would admit to using the television as a useful distraction from time to time. After all, if you're at home all day every day with a young child, you find yourself with a lot of hours to fill, and an hour or two in front of the television can certainly make life easier.

Bearing this in mind, most parents would agree that it's not realistic to impose a blanket ban, especially as children get older and want to talk to their friends about their favourite programmes. You may be reassured to know that if your child is aged between three and five years old, there is evidence to suggest that some television viewing can actually be beneficial and can aid reading and short-term memory skills. So allowing a child in this age group to watch a favourite television programme, provided it is age appropriate, is unlikely to be too much of a problem.

Insight

Instead of allowing your child to watch television in 'real time' think about recording their favourite programme or buying a DVD. This makes it easier to watch just one episode and makes watching television more of an event than a habit.

CURRENT GUIDELINES

If you are committed to getting your child more active, it's wise to pay attention to the current guidelines about television time. Young children should be discouraged from watching more than an hour to two of television each day and it isn't a good idea to allow your child to have a television in their room, as this makes it harder for you to monitor their viewing habits. If possible, it's far better for your child if you can watch and enjoy their favourite television programmes together. Not only will this help your child to learn as much as possible from the television, but it will also limit the amount that you are prepared to let them watch, as you will almost certainly get bored before they do.

If your child is under the age of two, then it really is best to limit television time to a maximum of 30 minutes to one hour per day. In recent years, several television shows have been developed which are aimed specifically at babies under one year old. In most cases these are little more than shots of babies and soothing music. Although your child may appear to find this fascinating viewing, studies suggest that they aren't able to understand and process what they see on the screen, so it doesn't teach them anything apart from how to watch television. Bear in mind that babies aren't able to watch television unless you turn it on and put them in front of it – so make the decision to keep it switched off for as long as you can. The sooner you introduce your baby to television, the harder it will be for you to limit their viewing habits as they grow.

If your child is already a toddler or pre-schooler, they may already be accustomed to watching a certain amount of television and may react badly if you suddenly change the rules. To avoid tantrums, the key is to gradually reduce the amount of television they watch – aim for five minutes less each day – until they are watching an acceptable amount. Be prepared to distract them with other games and activities, and aim to keep these as active as possible. If your child is able to turn the television on and off by themselves – many children acquire this skill at an early age – then consider unplugging it or switching it off at the wall, or installing a timer that will switch the television off when they have reached whatever viewing limit you choose to set. Alternatively, think about scheduling a time for them to watch a favourite programme or DVD and switch the television off as soon as it is finished. Within a week or two you should find they begin to adjust.

Case study: Television tantrums

The problem

Lauren is a three-year-old girl who has a tantrum every time her parents try to restrict the amount of television she watches. She started watching television sometime around her first birthday. At first it was easy to limit how much she watched, but by the time she turned two she was demanding to watch the same DVD over and over again. If her parents refused to let her watch, she would switch it on herself, and if they turned it off, she would throw a tantrum. After her third birthday it became clear that Lauren wasn't going to outgrow her fascination with the television, so her parents realized that they needed to take action.

The solution

Lauren never asked to watch television when she was out and about or busy doing other things, so her parents knew it was possible to distract her. They waited until summer when there was less chance of bad weather, and made an effort to take Lauren out every day. They went to toddler groups, played in the park, joined a music and dance group and met up with friends for play dates – anything that kept her away from the television.

When they were at home Lauren's parents found that it was possible to distract Lauren with other activities. So they started baking cakes together, painting pictures and modelling with Play Doh. At the end of every day, Lauren was allowed to watch her favourite television programme before bed, to help her wind down after her busy day.

The outcome

Although Lauren did ask to watch television at first, within a week she seemed to accept that she could only have 'TV time' once a day. For the first few days her parents made sure that the television was unplugged, so that she couldn't turn it on by herself, and although this caused a few tantrums, her parents stood their ground and distracted her with other activities. Lauren now watches very little television and is more likely to throw a tantrum if she doesn't get her daily trip to the park. As an unexpected bonus, her mum has lost the last of the baby weight she had been carrying since Lauren was born!

Activities for babies

When it comes to establishing an active lifestyle, you can't start soon enough. You might not realize it, but even small babies need regular exercise to help them build strength, use their muscles, improve motor skills and prepare for crawling and walking.

Unlike older children, babies don't need any special equipment or planned programme of activities. Of course, there are many toys and games that are specially designed for this purpose, but these are by no means essential. All that your baby really needs is the opportunity to develop strength – and this can only happen if they spend time out of the confines of a cot, pram or car seat and are encouraged to move about.

New parents often assume that their baby is safest when tucked inside a Moses basket, or strapped into a bouncy chair. In many respects this is true, but it's important for a baby to spend time on a playmat, folded towel or blanket too, particularly on their tummy. Now that guidelines recommend that babies should be put down to sleep on their backs to reduce the risk of Sudden Infant Death Syndrome (SIDS), some parents worry about placing their baby on their tummy at all. It doesn't help that many babies cry when placed on their front – but this is usually only because they are used to lying on their backs. Health professionals agree that 'tummy time' is the best way to help your baby develop head and neck strength, but close supervision is required as babies tire easily and will need to be picked up and turned over after a short time.

Once your baby can support the weight of their own head, the next step is developing upper body strength, which will enable them to sit up and, later, crawl.

Insight

If your baby screams when you put them on their front, think about putting them on the bed, rather that the floor. The softer surface seems to make babies happier – but make sure you supervise them closely so they don't roll off.

Encouraging your baby to reach out and touch toys or rattles and giving them the opportunity to learn how to stretch and roll will help to develop these early skills. From there, your baby will work on strengthening their legs and improving balance. Once these skills have been mastered, your baby will be ready to start walking.

Devoting a few minutes each day to these simple activities is the best way to help your baby become more active. You should be able to identify the times of day when your baby is most active, so set aside a few minutes for playtime during these periods. However, it's important not to push your baby into any of these activities. So if they seem tired, distressed or over-stimulated, stop for a while, have a cuddle and try again at a later date.

It's important to be guided by your baby's developmental stage, but do bear in mind that all babies are different, so there's no need to worry if your baby takes a little while longer to master some skills than others. If you are at all concerned, check with your health visitor or GP. The following suggestions should give you some idea of how to get started.

FROM BIRTH TO THREE MONTHS

You will notice lots of changes in your baby within the first three months. At just four weeks old, your baby may be able to follow a moving object with their eyes for a few seconds, and may even be able to lift their head slightly when lying face down on a mat. Soon after, babies tend to develop a fascination with their hands and feet, and love to spend time waving their arms and kicking their legs. By eight weeks old, some babies can reach out and grab for a toy.

In the early weeks and months, it's a good idea to place your baby on their tummy to help strengthen the neck and shoulder muscles. Placing them on a change mat or folded towel should make it more comfortable, or you could try a specially designed, padded baby gym, which often comes complete with safe mirrors, soft toys and rattles. Alternatively, try placing them in the middle of the bed. Be aware that babies often master new skills without parents realizing, so never leave your baby unsupervised on a bed, sofa or changing table in case they learn to roll off.

Insight

Babies don't need lots of toys, but it's a good idea to buy a couple with interesting sounds, colours or textures. Hold these in front of your baby to attract their attention and encourage them to reach out to touch them.

Babies also respond well to high contrast black, white and red toys that are easy for them to see even though their vision remains fuzzy. Toys that make a sound, such as rattles, are also appealing, but it's important to make sure that all toys are suitable for your baby's age, and are too big to fit in their mouth to prevent the risk of choking. Consider hanging a mobile over the baby's cot or changing table, and hold out interesting toys for them to grab or kick as this will help them to develop strength and coordination.

Babies of this age are often too young to benefit from any organized activities, but some parents find baby yoga classes to be a great way to bond with their baby – and many of them teach movements which can help to soothe colic, relieve sleep problems and improve digestion. Classes often include yoga moves for adults too, so they can be a good way for tired and stressed parents to relax.

Pre-school learning programmes such as Gymboree also run gym sessions that are suitable from birth. These focus on sensory exploration, tummy time and baby massage for infants up to six months old, progressing to more active sessions including music and art for toddlers and pre-schoolers. If you're interested in organized classes, this is a great way to get your baby used to taking part in activities, as the curriculum and available classes change in line with your baby's age and developmental skills.

Tummy time

My health visitor told me that it was important to give Sam some 'tummy time' every day, so that he could build up the strength he would need to support the weight of his head. The first time I tried he screamed the house down, and I was very nervous about him lying face down on the mat in case he found it difficult to breathe. After a few more failed attempts, I asked a friend for advice. She suggested putting him down on a padded baby gym and surrounding him with a few toys and a safe plastic mirror to encourage him to lift his head. This was more successful, but it wasn't until I bought a small plastic mat, which could be filled with water, that he really started to enjoy it. Once it was topped up with water, lots of colourful shapes floated around inside the mat, and Sam was fascinated. We had tummy time like this for about five minutes, two or three times each day and he got very excited every time he saw his special mat.

Joanne is mum to Sam, six months.

FROM THREE TO SIX MONTHS

By the age of three months many babies have learned how to roll from their side to their back. Once they have mastered this, they will quickly learn how to roll from their back to their side, and later over on to their front. During this stage of development, babies usually learn how to prop themselves up and lift their head while lying on their tummy, and can sometimes sit with support.

At this stage, it's vital to continue with regular tummy time, as this will help your baby to strengthen the muscles needed for crawling and walking. As soon as your baby is able to support their head, surround them with soft pillows and encourage them to sit on your lap or propped up against cushions. Some parents buy specially designed, moulded seats, which can be introduced when your baby is three or four months old. These can help your baby to strengthen the muscles needed to sit unsupported – and give them a whole new perspective on the world. At first, take care to only use this kind of seat for a few minutes at a time as your baby will become tired very easily.

Many parents choose to take their baby swimming for the first time at the age of three to four months old – although you can start much earlier – and some swimming pools offer special parent and baby swimming classes. A 2007 survey by the Swimming Teachers' Association (STA) showed an 84 per cent increase in the number of babies having swimming lessons since 2005. They estimate that more than 300,000 babies and toddlers in the UK are now taking classes, so you should have no problem finding some in your area.

Classes usually take place in training or hydrotherapy pools that are heated to a higher temperature, as most public pools are too cold for small babies. The water should be at least 32°C for babies under 12 weeks or under 12 lb, and 30°C for a baby over 12 weeks or over 12 lb. If you don't want to enrol in classes, which can be expensive, or if there isn't a suitable pool in your area, you could buy a special baby wetsuit, which can help keep your baby warm in the water for short periods of time.

At this stage, the objective is to ensure that your baby is happy and confident in the water, so focus on having fun. Classes range from simple splashing around, to more structured sessions where babies can learn to swim through hoops, ride on floats and support themselves by holding on to the side.

All you need is a swim nappy and suitable bathing suit, but if you're not taking part in classes, you might like to take a small ball or plastic toy into the water for your baby to play with.

The NHS immunization information advises that babies can be taken swimming before the primary immunizations. However, you should ensure you take care to dispose of soiled nappies and observe good hygiene as in any other public place.

Insight

It's important to help your baby to be confident in water, so you can do lots of preparation at home in the bath. Buy stacking cups to pour water, and encourage your baby to kick and splash.

Did you know?

Up to the age of about 18 months, a baby's epiglottis will automatically close over and block the throat when it is submerged in water. This means that it's safe for a properly supervised baby to go underwater for a few seconds – although some instructors prefer not to do this as they think it can be traumatic for the baby.

Swimming for babies

I started taking Sophie to swimming lessons when she was four months old. I had been thinking about taking her to the pool for a while, but wasn't sure what we should be doing and felt that I needed some guidance. The classes were fun for both of us. I held Sophie in my arms, sometimes lying flat in the water and sometimes lying back on my shoulder. We spent a lot of time singing songs, splashing water and playing with toys like balls and plastic boats.

By the time she was 18 months old, Sophie loved standing on the side of the pool and jumping into the water. She learned how to swim before she started school and is now a very confident swimmer. I'm sure that's because we started lessons when she was a baby.

Richard is dad to Sophie, seven.

FROM SIX TO NINE MONTHS

The biggest physical changes occur in the second half of a baby's first year, which means there are lots more games and physical activities you can explore together. Some babies learn to sit without support when they are six or seven months old, and can often reach for favourite toys and 'rake' them closer. Continue to stimulate your baby with brightly coloured or noisy toys, but encourage them to reach out and grab their favourites while sitting on your lap. They will soon be able to pass toys from one hand to the other and may even bang them together to make a noise – these activities will improve their strength and help to develop hand–eye coordination. They may also enjoy throwing a toy on the floor and waiting for you to pick it up, only to throw it back down again, which is good exercise for you, if not for them!

At six months, some babies can cover lots of ground simply by rolling around on the floor. Even if they are not yet on the move, babies of this age will enjoy any activities that help to strengthen their legs in preparation for crawling and walking. This is the time when many parents buy baby bouncers, which can be fixed to door frames allowing a baby to 'stand' upright and bounce up and down. Baby walkers are also popular, as these allow babies to scoot around the room on wheels. However, these can cause accidents so it's vital to supervise your baby closely at all times, particularly on wood floors – where they can pick up quite a bit of speed – and in areas where toys or other items have been left on the floor, as this could cause the walker to tip up. They should never be used near stairways, and you may find it safer to use a stationary walker or exerciser, or lock the wheels in place instead. This type of equipment shouldn't be used for more than about

30 minutes each day, broken up into five- or ten-minute sessions. Babies get bored and tired very quickly, so if they start to cry or complain it's time to stop.

By eight months, some babies start pulling themselves up to standing and will need little encouragement to get on their feet. If your baby is keen to be upright, then give them lots of help and encouragement to stand and applaud their efforts every time. Their next challenge is learning how to walk, so make sure that you are their biggest cheerleader and encourage them to practise as much as they want to.

Baby bouncers

Taylor loves his baby bouncer. We fitted it to the top of the door frame in our living room and he spends a few minutes bouncing up and down in it every day. He loves to kick his legs and wave his arms around but he gets tired after a few minutes, so we don't leave him in it for long.

Emma is mum to Taylor, five months.

FROM NINE TO TWELVE MONTHS

Many babies are on the move before their first birthday: most will be able to roll around or scoot on their bottoms, many will be crawling and some may even be walking independently. Crawling and walking requires strength and coordination, so your baby will need lots of practice and is likely to experience a few bumps and scrapes along the way.

If your baby shows signs of being ready to crawl, place a soft blanket or duvet on the floor and tempt your baby to crawl to the other side to reach a favourite toy. Alternatively, roll a ball and encourage them to follow it to the other side of the mat. Proficient crawlers may also enjoy the opportunity to crawl through large cardboard boxes or fabric tunnels. In warm weather your baby will enjoy playing these kinds of games in the garden. Just be sure to stick to safe, grassy areas until they are steady on their feet.

Before they learn to walk, many babies learn how to pull themselves up using furniture and 'cruise' around the room. If your baby shows signs of being ready to do this, remove any breakables, secure heavy objects and make sure that your baby can't reach out for anything that could cause injury. As soon as they appear interested, help your baby to pull up to a standing position and practise walking while holding on to your hands. This is a good time to buy push or pull toys such as toy carts or trolleys, as these will help your baby to balance as they take their first steps.

As they approach their first birthday, many babies begin to imitate the activities they see you perform on a daily basis. So you may find that your child is keen to 'help' with the housework. Any activity of this kind should be encouraged – and if you're aware that you spend too much time sitting down, now is a good time to rethink your habits before your child has the opportunity to adopt your sedentary lifestyle.

Babies of this age often respond well to music, so you may find that joining a baby and toddler music group will encourage them to dance and move about. Alternatively, you could practise singing songs such as 'Head, Shoulders, Knees and Toes' or 'The Wheels on the Bus' and encourage your child to copy the actions. This is a great way to introduce your child to music and dance and will also help to improve coordination.

Babies of this age love to dance too, so turn on your favourite music, pick them up and dance around the room, or hold their hands and encourage them to bounce to the beat.

Insight

Ride-on toys are popular with this age group, and some baby trikes are sturdy enough to use in place of a pushchair for short trips to the shops or the park. Make sure that your child is securely strapped in, and look for one with a comfortable handle, so that you can push them along.

Music groups

I started taking Suki to music classes when she was four months old. Even though she was too young to participate, she seemed to enjoy the music and it got us both out of the house. By the time she turned one she had started doing the actions to some of the songs and loved banging the drums and playing with the maracas. Now she's walking she's started to dance along and can do the actions to some of the songs.

Natalie is mum to 18-month-old Suki.

Activities for toddlers

The toddler years cover the period between the first and third birthdays. This is the time when your little one is growing from baby to child, when they are fighting for independence and control and may throw a tantrum if they don't get their own way. The typical toddler is a bundle of energy, so you shouldn't have to try too hard to encourage them to be active. In fact, if you are prepared to create plenty of opportunities for physical games and activities, they will be more than willing participants.

Safety is the most important consideration when introducing your toddler to new games and activities. Toddlers are particularly fearless and have no sense of danger. They love to climb, run and jump and will often set themselves challenges that are still beyond their physical capabilities. In most circumstances, they will continue to practise until they perfect a new skill. This means that they will sometimes attempt to copy older children and do things that are beyond their capabilities. Climbing and balancing could prove particularly risky, as toddlers tend not to recognize their own limitations, so it's important to keep a close eye on them at all times.

Even at this tender age, it's sometimes possible to identify where your toddler's particular interests lie. Some children love to run, others start to climb as soon as they can stand, and many love to dance or jump. Most are interested in all of them equally! Although it's important to encourage your toddler to try out all kinds of activities, observing your child's physical predilections should make it easier for you to not only find activities that will interest them, but also to identify areas of your home that may need extra childproofing. For instance, a child who loves to climb may be at risk of heavy furniture or unsecured bookshelves falling on top of them if they try to scale them – which they will almost certainly do. But you can indulge their love of climbing by taking them to a soft play area or playground where they can safely climb without risk of injury. You could also think about buying a small, age-appropriate activity centre, which can be used indoors or outdoors. Many of these can be adapted for use as your child grows, so should be a sound investment for years to come.

If your toddler is keen on jumping, think about getting a small child-size trampoline. This might prevent your child from jumping on beds, which can cause injury if they fall off. Opt for one that has been designed with toddlers in mind – these are often little more than 50 cm in diameter and have a sturdy handle that your child can hold on to as they jump.

Children who love to run will be easily amused by chasing games or trips to the park with friends, so discourage running around the house by taking regular trips to safe areas where your toddler can run off all their energy. Or, if you have outdoor space, your toddler might enjoy playing ball games instead.

Although current guidelines suggest that toddlers should get at least 30 minutes a day of physical activity, you might find it more helpful to think about your toddler's day as a whole. At this age, children have energy to spare, and should be on the go pretty much all the time. So, aside from daily naps, make sure that your toddler is always moving around, and try to avoid long periods in front of the television or strapped into a buggy.

On rainy days, you may find it useful to take your toddler to a playgroup or parent and child activity group. This gives them a great opportunity to interact with other children and gain access to toys and equipment that you may not have at home. It's also a good idea to stock up on 'active' toys and games for days when you can't play outside. Look for anything that requires your child to move about, such as battery-operated mats which make noises when your child walks across them, mini vacuum cleaners, brushes and mops and ride-on toys. You might also find it useful to get hold of a couple of CDs of children's music, so that you can sing and dance along and practise the actions with your child.

However, try not to be too put off by bad weather. Unless it is particularly cold or stormy, most children love playing outside in the rain. Just make sure your child has a pair of wellies and a raincoat, and possibly even a fun umbrella – then head outside and spend some time splashing in the puddles.

Rainy days

It's very tempting to stay indoors when the weather is bad, but I find this is usually a recipe for a disastrous day. Joshua gets very hyperactive if he's cooped up indoors all day and needs to burn off some energy, so unless the weather is really bad, we go outside regardless. He loves jumping through puddles and getting muddy – and the playground is always nice and quiet when it's raining!

Claire is mum to Joshua, age two.

Activities for pre-schoolers

Between the ages of three and five, children are more able to follow instructions, so there are lots of new ways that you can play together that will keep them fit and active. Like toddlers, pre-schoolers enjoy physical play, and find it almost impossible to sit still. Unlike toddlers, they are now more interested in playing with other children, so this is the perfect time to encourage play dates. This is a great solution for parents who are short of time, as it means you can take it in turns with other parents to supervise trips to the park or invite their friends over to your house and encourage them to run around and play.

Insight

Soft play-centres are a great place for children to get some exercise. Most towns now have one, and many are reasonably priced – especially if you take out membership. Get together with other parents and arrange a regular outing, then you can share the transport too.

At this stage in development, you will be able to play proper games with your child for the first time. Show them how to play traditional playground games such as hopscotch, tag and follow my leader, and take time to practise throwing or kicking a ball and playing catch. Your child's coordination and balance is also improving, so set up an obstacle course and challenge them to race around it. An outdoor course could include climbing over or under climbing frames, crawling through boxes or fabric tunnels, balancing or hopping on one leg, jumping, bouncing a ball, using a hula hoop or skipping. Simple games such as hide and seek, treasure hunts or even building a fort can also boost your child's activity levels, and are lots of fun too.

If you have a garden, then you could encourage your child to help you out with simple chores. Child-size wheelbarrows and garden tools can be bought fairly cheaply, and your pre-schooler will probably enjoy watering plants and helping with – or copying – your garden chores or digging in the dirt. You could also section off a small area of the garden for your child to grow flowers or vegetables. Start out with seeds that germinate quickly, so that your child won't have to wait too long before the first green shoots appear.

When the weather is warm, inflatable paddling pools filled either with water or plastic balls can be great fun, and running through sprinklers and playing in a sandpit can create an exciting holiday atmosphere in your own garden.

This is the age when most children show some interest in riding bikes or scooters or even basic roller skates, so encourage their interest by getting hold of an age-appropriate bike or scooter and teaching them how to ride it safely. For more on this, see Chapter 3.

From the age of four, many clubs and classes are available to children, so you could think about enrolling your child in any that appeal. Dance classes are often a popular choice for girls, and the cute frilly costumes and shoes are often all the incentive they need to get moving. Don't assume that boys won't be interested in dance classes too. It's very common for pre-school boys to enjoy this kind of activity, so don't laugh or try to talk them out of it if they show any interest.

By the age of three or four, most children are ready to leave parent and child swimming classes behind and join pre-school classes instead. Some parents find the idea of their child getting into the water without them quite worrying, but provided that your child is happy to join in and you are confident that the teacher is fully qualified, then you should have no cause for concern. Alternatively, try to make time for a weekly swimming trip. At this stage you can move the focus to teaching your child how to swim rather than just splashing around, so encourage them to kick their legs and move their arms, and use armbands and floats for extra buoyancy while they learn.

Although some organized sports clubs may be open to children as young as four or five, team sports are best avoided until your child is around the age of six. Experts maintain that it's best not to encourage your child to specialize in one particular sport at this age, and children of this age often don't have the necessary concentration or coordination to play team sports. That's not to say that they shouldn't practise skills such as kicking a ball into a goal, throwing and catching and hitting a soft ball with a bat. These skills are the foundation of most team games, and learning them now will develop their skills and boost your child's confidence before they start playing them at school.

By the age of three or four, most children are out of their pushchair or buggy, so you should resist the temptation to use the car for short journeys and encourage them to walk instead. Don't be surprised if your child announces that they are tired within the first five minutes and asks to be carried. Going for a walk isn't very appealing to a young child, but it's easy to find ways to make it more enjoyable. If they have a bike or scooter, suggest that they ride that instead, or push their doll in a pushchair. Suggest a trip to the playground or a visit to a friend's house after you have walked round the park, so that they have some motivation to keep going, and vary your pace and route so that they are less likely to get bored. Suggest that you run, hop, skip or jump – and challenge your child to race you to the next tree to keep things varied.

Insight

If you have a baby and a pre-schooler, consider swapping your double buggy for a pushchair with a 'buggy board'. This means that your older child can walk until they get tired, then stand on the board and ride the rest of the way.

Nature walks

Like many parents, we have found it difficult to get our children to come with us for a walk – within a few minutes they always want to go home or ask to be carried. That's when we decided to turn our walks into more of an event. Now we drive out into the county and go on nature walks instead. We take a picnic and stop to point out animals and birds and look out for certain flowers and trees. The girls are getting some great exercise, and they are learning too.

Francesca is mum to Rose, four, and Martha, five.

Playing safe

No matter how careful you are, accidents can – and will – happen. Young children haven't yet developed good balance and coordination, and lack the judgement to know when they are putting themselves at risk, so it's very important to make sure that they are supervised at all times. The following tips should help you to keep your child safe.

▶ *Make sure that all toys and games have passed the relevant safety checks, and bear the CE or Lion Mark to prove it. You should also check that toys are suitable for your child's age group, and that all bikes, scooters or skates are well maintained and safe to ride. It is recommended that protective helmets, knee and elbow pads should be worn when your child is playing with these kinds of toys.*

▶ *If you are taking your child to the playground, look for one that has soft surfaces, sand or wooden chips under all equipment so that your child is less likely to get hurt if they fall off. Teach your child the importance of using handrails when they climb on and off equipment, and explain why they shouldn't run in front of swings that other children are using or go down the slide until other children have stepped aside.*

▶ *Ensure that your child wears sunscreen and a sun hat when playing outside in warm, sunny weather, and try to limit the time they spend in the sun during the hottest part of the day.*

▶ *Make sure that you have a first-aid kit with antiseptic cream and wipes, bandages and plasters, so that you can quickly attend to any bumps and scrapes. You might find that plasters decorated with your child's favourite cartoon characters or ice packs that you can keep in the fridge to apply to bumps will help to soothe your child more quickly if they take a tumble.*

10 THINGS TO REMEMBER

1 *It's never too soon to encourage your child to get active. Even babies benefit from regular, strength-building exercise.*

2 *Limiting television time is a good idea. Don't allow young children to get into the habit of watching more than one hour of television each day – once they get into the habit of doing this they will be less inclined to get active.*

3 *If your child can turn the television on by themselves, turn it off at the wall or install a timer to limit how much they can watch.*

4 *Babies benefit from regular 'tummy time' as this helps them to develop the upper body strength they will need to sit, crawl and walk.*

5 *Unless your local swimming pool is heated to 32°C (for babies under 12 weeks or 12 lb), or 30°C (for babies over 12 weeks or 12 lb), your child should wear a wetsuit to keep them warm.*

6 *Small indoor trampolines are a great way for toddlers to get some exercise. These usually have a sturdy handle and are much safer than bouncing on the bed!*

7 *Team sports are best avoided until your child is six, as younger children seldom have the necessary coordination or concentration to play.*

8 *Encourage your child to practice kicking, throwing, catching and hitting, as this will teach them the basics of most sports they will play at school.*

9 *Remember that young children have poor balance and coordination, and find it hard to gauge risk – so make sure they are supervised at all times.*

10 *Protective helmets, knee and elbow pads should always be used when your child is using bikes, scooters or skates.*

5

....

Making exercise fun

In this chapter you will learn:
- *how to make fitness fun*
- *how to build your child's confidence*
- *why active holidays and sports camps could help your child get fit.*

Regardless of age or ability, keeping fit should be fun. Unfortunately, for a significant proportion of adults and children, taking regular exercise is anything but. Later in this chapter you will find plenty of suggestions on fun ways to get fit, but first it's important to examine the reasons why you and/or your child don't enjoy being active.

If you are a reluctant participant in sports or activities, try to remember when you first started feeling this way. It's very likely that you have felt this way since your schooldays. No matter how successful we may be in other areas of our lives, many of us simply accept that we are not the 'sporty type' because of experiences we had in school PE lessons. Children can be very cruel, and the memories of being the last to be picked in games, or limping in at last place at school sports day are memories that can – and do – stay with us for life.

If we come to the conclusion as children that sport and exercise is not for us, it becomes very difficult to challenge this notion as we get older. Admittedly, as adults we may make the effort to get fit – usually as part of a weight-loss programme – but this usually involves boring, repetitive gym visits, jogging through built-up areas which are thick with traffic fumes, or doing laps around the park. This isn't most people's idea of fun and, as a result, it is usually very difficult to sustain. In fact, for many people, exercise is more like a punishment than a pleasure, which only serves to reinforce the belief that we are not 'sporty'. With this in mind, is it any wonder that we struggle to make a lasting commitment to keep fit?

If you recognize any of the scenarios set out above, then it's very important to find a way to break the pattern and ensure that your child doesn't end up with the same negative associations towards sports and activities. This will inevitably mean that you will have to challenge your own ideas about exercise, and the only way to do this is to convince your child – and yourself – that keeping fit can be fun.

Insight

If you have bad memories or experiences of sports and exercise, make a resolution not to communicate these to your child. They will only learn to associate keeping fit with having fun if you make a point to present activities as a treat, rather than a chore.

If your child is not a natural athlete, it's very likely that they will already be demonstrating some reluctance to take part in organized sports or team games. Moreover, if they have been teased at school because they can't run fast or catch, hit or kick a ball with ease, they are likely to be so sensitive about their perceived lack of sporting ability that they are unwilling to try any new sports. If you had a similar experience at school yourself, it's very tempting to let them off the hook, tell them not to worry and focus their energies on other – usually sedentary – interests instead. However, this will only reinforce your child's belief that sporting activities are not for them. Having said that, neither should you turn it into a big issue and nag them to practise and improve their skills. The best tactic is to identify an activity that they can have fun with – or even better, one that you can enjoy together – and take it from there. Later in this chapter you will find more ideas on how to do this, but first you need to take a few minutes to explore exactly what it is that you and your family don't like about sport and physical activities.

What's stopping you from getting fit?

Think about the things you really enjoy whether it's reading, shopping, cooking, socializing with friends, watching television or going to the cinema. Whatever your particular hobby or interest, there's a good chance that you find the time to indulge in it at least once a week – or even once a day.

Next, try to identify what it is about these things that you enjoy. For instance, if you enjoy reading it could be because books help you to escape from the demands of daily life, teach you new things or help you to relax. If you love to spend your Saturday afternoons shopping, then try to identify what appeals to you. Is it that you enjoy shopping for new clothes that make you look great, or buying new things for the house to make it more comfortable or beautifully decorated? If you enjoy cooking, perhaps it's because you enjoy looking after your friends and family, or simply because you love eating delicious food. Or perhaps it's because you want to practise and improve your skills or want to impress your friends with your culinary talents.

Now think about taking part in sport or physical activities. Try to identify what it is that puts you off. More specifically, what excuses do you make to yourself when you're looking to find a reason for not being more active? It's likely that some of the following reasons will sound familiar:

- ▶ *I'm too tired.*
- ▶ *I'm too fat/unfit.*
- ▶ *It's too wet/cold.*
- ▶ *I don't have time.*
- ▶ *I can't afford it.*

- *It's too difficult.*
- *There's nothing to do or nowhere to exercise in my neighbourhood.*
- *I'll look stupid.*
- *I'm no good at it.*
- *I'll start tomorrow/next week/month/year.*

Next, think about the hobby or pastime that you enjoy and imagine applying any of these excuses to that activity. For example, if you were planning to read a book, you might not let being too tired put you off – you would probably just read a page instead of a chapter. Or perhaps you would read more the next day to make up for it. As anyone who has stayed up half the night to finish a real page-turner will testify, no matter how busy you are you can always find time. And if you don't have the money for new books, you would probably borrow them from a library or from friends.

Insight

As a parent, you are already an expert at shooting down your child's well-used excuses, so think about how to deal with your own. If you don't want to go outside in the cold or wet, make sure you have an activity such as a fitness DVD or active computer game that you can play at home. If you're too tired, promise yourself that you'll reward yourself with a bubble bath and a good book if you go out for that walk. Preparing responses to your own – and your child's – excuses will make it easier to motivate yourself and get active.

Although it may seem like a waste of time, taking a few minutes to examine what motivates us to do the things we enjoy – and what makes it easy for us to talk ourselves out of doing the things we don't – can really help you to revolutionize your family's approach to fitness. This can not only reveal how you always manage to find the time, energy and opportunity to do the things you enjoy, but it can also help you to identify exactly what it is that you enjoy about your preferred pastimes. For example, if you enjoy shopping for new clothes because you like to keep up with fashion, look good and receive admiring glances from others, you might find that trying out a new fitness regime, which is endorsed by some celebrities who are feted for their glamorous appearance, might appeal. And if you find that your most frequently used excuses relate to not having time, or being put off by the weather, then you could be most suited to activities that you can practise from your own home so that you don't have to waste any time on travel.

> **Insight**
>
> Don't put off until tomorrow the things that you can do today! Reading this book indicates that you intend to help your child to get fit, so stop making excuses and get started right away. Turn off the television and go for a walk – the sooner you get started, the sooner you'll get fit.

Once you have tried this approach on yourself, do the same for your child. You may well be surprised by some of their answers. Perhaps you will discover that their reluctance to take part in sports may be because they don't think it's 'cool' to be sporty. It could be that they are worried that they won't be any good and other children will laugh at them. Or perhaps they are self-conscious about their changing body and don't like wearing shorts or swimwear. You could even find that they are resistant to going swimming because they don't want to mess up their hair!

It's very important to take all your child's worries and anxieties very seriously, no matter how trivial they may seem to you. Make a list of all your child's concerns, and then use this information to work out a list of solutions, or ways that you can make sport and activities fun for you and your family. For example, if your child says that they don't like exercising outside in cold or wet weather, suggest indoor alternatives such as badminton or dancing. If your child is overweight and admits that exercise makes them uncomfortable or breathless, start with low-impact activities such as walking – but take time to work out an interesting route or a fun destination to keep them going. Or if your child isn't confident enough to enjoy team games, think about gymnastics or martial arts, where they can develop their skills at their own pace.

Despite your efforts, bear in mind that your child probably will complain and do all they can to get out of it. Your job is to make it as easy and enjoyable as possible for them to get fit, but there comes a point when you will have to be firm and make it clear that they can't get out of it completely. Stick with each activity for at least a few sessions to see if you can get them to a point where they can start having fun. This could take minutes, weeks or months – but once they start to enjoy themselves, you can give yourself a pat on the back because you have reached an important milestone: your family has started to have fun with fitness.

Don't overdo it

Many of us avoid taking regular exercise simply because it feels too much like hard work! Of course, if you want to improve your family's fitness, then you will have to make sure that everyone is putting in enough effort. But that's no excuse to push yourself or your child too hard. Pain, discomfort or dizziness is your body's way of telling you that you are overdoing it. If you or your child experience any of these symptoms, then get checked out by a doctor, just to be sure that it's safe to continue.

Case study: Showing your child that fitness can be fun

The problem

Jasmine is an 11-year-old girl who keeps coming up with excuses to get out of PE. When she started year six she became increasingly reluctant to take part in PE lessons. Her teachers told Jasmine's parents, Sian and Leon, that she put in very little effort and often asked to be excused from class because she felt unwell. Until then, Jasmine always seemed to enjoy PE, and although she didn't play in any of the school teams, she was a popular and able student. She also told her parents that she wanted to give up the ballet classes which she had enjoyed since she was six years old, and started to

(Contd)

spend much of her free time in her bedroom, listening to music or chatting to her friends on MSN.

The solution

Jasmine's parents' attempts to coerce their daughter into being more active fell on deaf ears. She claimed that she had too much homework to keep up with dance classes, and dismissed school sports as 'stupid'. After checking with a few of her friends' parents, it became clear that most of Jasmine's friends shared her attitude. Her peers were interested in clothes, music, boys and celebrity gossip but thought that sport was boring and thought that any girls who took part in it were 'sad'.

Jasmine's parents realized that she wasn't going to agree to any activity unless it seemed suitably grown up. They explained the situation to her ballet teacher who said that lots of girls of Jasmine's age rejected the discipline of ballet and suggested that she might prefer to learn some different styles of dance instead. When they looked through the classes available at their local dance school Jasmine became very excited at the prospect of taking lessons in street dance as she thought it would be a great way to impress her friends at parties.

The outcome

Jasmine's parents enrolled her in street dance classes on the condition that she stopped missing school PE lessons, and promised that she could sign up for an extra class if she kept to her side of the bargain. She now takes hip-hop dance classes too, and some of her friends also enrolled. They now practise together most days after school.

Winning and losing

If you enjoy sports yourself but your child doesn't, you probably find their lack of interest or ability hard to understand. Although this is somewhat less common than the scenario detailed on pages 74–5, it is by no means unusual. What many fit and active parents fail to understand – particularly if they excel at sports themselves – is that their expertise, and the competitiveness that usually goes along with it, can be intimidating to their children.

If your child grows up absorbing the message that it's important to excel, to win and to be the best, they may find it easier to opt out of sports than risk disappointing you, especially if they have not inherited your natural aptitude. Generally speaking, children like to win – but it's a rare child who has the ability to come first every time. If your child grows up thinking that winning is more important than taking part, they will have very little incentive to join in – unless they are certain that they can be the best – and will often give up on new sports or activities if they don't feel that they are 'good enough'.

Insight

Make it a priority to support your child when they participate in sporting events – even if you're not a sports fan. Standing on the sidelines sends a message that what they are doing is important and worthwhile, and shows that you are proud of their achievements. Regardless of the outcome, always praise their efforts and focus on one or two things that they did particularly well, or ways that they have improved. This takes the focus off winning and losing but still helps them to develop pride in their achievements.

Anyone who enjoys playing in a Saturday morning football league, swims regularly or takes a weekly yoga class usually does so because they enjoy it, find it relaxing or recognize that it is a great way to relieve stress. Being the best shouldn't influence the decision to take part, so it's important to teach our children that enjoying sport can be its own reward.

Of course, this can be easier said than done. If you enjoy sports yourself, it is only natural that you would want to encourage your child to share your enthusiasm. However, pushing your child to take part in activities that they don't enjoy can have the opposite effect and can put your child off sports for the rest of their life.

If you have been guilty of this, take some time to think about activities that might be more appealing to your child, and make a resolution to save your competitive spirit for times when you are playing sports with other adults or practising by yourself. Healthy competition is a good thing, but it doesn't help to encourage this in a child who is already unsure of their abilities. It's more important to focus on developing your child's strengths rather than seeking to eradicate their weaknesses. Most importantly, where you child is concerned you should forget about being the best and focus on having the most fun.

Focus on your child's enjoyment

Just because you enjoy a particular sport, that's no reason to assume that your child will feel the same way. When you're choosing activities for your child, remind yourself that you are catering to their interests, not yours – so don't pressure them to take part in activities that they don't enjoy or aren't very good at. Bear in mind that some children won't openly object to taking part in sports they don't like, usually because they want to please their sporty parents or gain their approval. For this reason, it's best to encourage them to try out a range of sports and activities before allowing them to settle on one or two that they like best – and try not to influence their decision. Above all, don't be surprised or disapproving if your daughter wants to play football and your son wants to study ballet. Keep an open mind and remind yourself that as long as your child is keeping active in one way or another, you don't need to worry.

Case study: How to ignite your child's interest in sport

The problem

Milo is an eight-year-old boy who resists his father's attempts to get him involved in sports. Milo's father, Duncan, enjoys sport both as a spectator and a participant. He plays tennis and golf on a regular basis, and Milo's 13-year-old brother, Theo, plays rugby and cricket for his school. Everyone expected Milo to follow in their footsteps, and has found it hard to understand his lack of interest.

The solution

Milo has spent a great deal of time watching his brother play in school matches, and often accompanies his dad to the tennis court or golf course. Although his intentions are good, Milo's father often spends too much time teaching his son the perfect technique rather than letting him play. He also asks Milo to be his ball boy or caddy on a fairly regular basis, so up to now his experience of sport has been rather boring.

Milo's father was so used to his older son taking part in organized sports that he forgot that a child of Milo's age doesn't have the concentration span to be interested in lots of rules, and watching someone else play – even an older brother – can become quite tedious.

The outcome

After taking some time to focus on the sport that Milo enjoys most – football – and organizing regular kickabouts in the park, it emerged that Milo does enjoy sport and is a very able player, but he needed to be allowed to learn at his own pace, without pressure, and he required some extra attention and support to build his confidence in his own ability.

Building confidence

In time, you may find that your child benefits from practising and refining the sporting skills that form the backbone of PE lessons, and the best ways to do this are detailed in the following chapter. But unless your child specifically asks for your help or is already showing a definite interest in a particular sport or activity, this is not the best way to start. Your child may already be sensitive about their performance in school sports and could have already made up their mind that they are 'no good' at them. Rather than trying to challenge this assumption directly, you will probably find it easier to start with something completely new, about which your child has no negative preconceptions.

No matter what activity you decide is best for your child, the most important thing is to give them your full support. Always focus on their strengths rather than their weaknesses, remind of them of what they can do instead of what they can't and make an effort to celebrate every achievement, no matter how small. If your child requires transport, then make an effort to do this without complaint, and try to be a willing and interested spectator as often as you possibly can.

CREATING A SENSE OF ACHIEVEMENT

It's very important to celebrate every goal that your child achieves, so that they have a sense that they are making good progress. They will almost certainly gain confidence as their skills and abilities improve, so in time this should help to motivate them to continue. But, at first, they may need a little more encouragement from you.

When you begin a new activity with your child, make sure that you are setting realistic goals so that it won't be too difficult for them to succeed. Don't expect or demand too much of your child to begin with, particularly if they are new to exercise, as this may make it too physically demanding and off-putting.

At first you may find that it helps to offer your child rewards, but be very careful with this as it can be counterproductive. Don't send mixed messages by rewarding your child with unhealthy snacks or more television time. Instead, think about promising them some new kit or equipment for their chosen activity provided they stick with it for a set period of time or attain a measurable (and achievable) goal. For example, your child may respond well to the promise of new trainers if they keep up their new activity, or if your child is overweight, it may work well to offer to buy them new clothes as their weight begins to stabilize.

Most parents are well aware that a little bit of bribery can work wonders with children, but don't feel that promising shopping trips or presents is the only – or the most effective – way to motivate your child. Inviting friends around for a sleepover or allowing them to help you choose the location for a family day out can also be used as incentives. Younger children may respond well to progress charts, especially if they are rewarded with a sticker every time they complete a particular activity. Helping your child to mark every goal that they reach will help to boost their confidence and increase their enjoyment of their chosen activity. This, in turn, will keep them interested enough to set their sights on the next goal and inspire them to keep practising.

After a while you should find that participating in a fun activity is its own reward, so try to gradually reduce these external incentives as time goes by. Your ultimate aim is for your child to keep fit and active because they enjoy the activities they participate in, not because they have their eye on another shopping trip or gold star!

Make your own progress chart

If your child is under the age of ten, you may find that drawing up a fitness chart will help to keep them motivated. List the days of the week in a column down the left side of the page, then list all the activities that they participate in across the top of the page. You could include activities such as going to the playground, walking to school, a family bike ride or a swim. Use stickers to show which activities your child has participated in each day, and then award them a gold star if they cover every activity in the list over the course of a week. To boost their motivation you could promise them a treat if they get four gold stars in a row.

Top ten fun activities

Children find all kinds of different activities enjoyable, depending on their interests and abilities. However, as a general rule, activities that are not considered to be particularly sporty – or anything that isn't usually taught in PE lessons – tend to be more appealing to a child who is not particularly active. For younger children, try to think in terms of playing rather than exercising and focus on silly games that keep them active. Older children, on the other hand, often respond well to anything that seems exciting or glamorous – so think in terms of encouraging a new grown-up in a new hobby. The following suggestions should help you to identify a fun activity for your child, irrespective of their age or ability.

DANCING

Children as young as 18 months to two years old can be enrolled in basic dance classes to give them a simple introduction to music and rhythm. Classes for toddlers often involve parent participation and the use of props such as ribbons, hula hoops, pompoms and maracas to help little ones develop coordination and creativity.

For older children, dancing is a great way to build strength and flexibility, improve posture and boost confidence. Most dance studios offer classes in ballet, tap and disco for children aged five and up – and some teach ballet to children as young as three. There are many more options including ballroom, jazz and modern for children over the age of six. For more information on dance classes, turn to Chapter 8.

However, you don't have to enrol your child in classes to enjoy dance – simply turn up the radio and encourage your child to move to the music. On rainy days you could even push back the furniture and have a disco at home – or you could really make an event of it and buy a karaoke machine, taking it in turns to perform your favourite songs, complete with dance moves.

TWISTER

Twister has been a popular family game since the 1960s and it's a great, fun way to get the family off the sofa. Most parents will remember Twister from their own childhood, but for those who don't, the game is played on a large plastic mat that is spread out on the floor. The mat is covered in four rows of red, blue, yellow and green circles. Players take turns to spin a dial, which tells them where to put their hands and feet, e.g. left foot red, right hand blue. Players are usually required to put themselves in awkward positions, and are eliminated if they fall or if their elbow or knee touches the mat. If adults and children are playing Twister together, it's important to take care that an adult doesn't fall on top of a child and hurt them. For this reason, it's best to limit play to two players at a time, or make sure that adults and children play separately.

DOG WALKING

Most children will ask if they can have a dog at some point, and many parents are understandably reluctant to agree to it. Pet ownership is a big commitment and should always be given careful consideration. It takes a great deal of time and money to take good care of a dog, but this can teach your child a sense of responsibility and also be a great way to get them active.

Even small dogs require regular exercise and need to be taken out for a walk at least once a day. Children are also inclined to run around and play with a dog, and playing ball games with their four-legged friend can improve their throwing ability.

Depending on their age and where you live, you might have to accompany your child on walks, so it's an activity that you can enjoy together. Many parents also find that walking a dog is a good way to get children out of the habit of expecting to be ferried everywhere by car. Your child is much more likely to agree to walking to school, to the shops or even to the park if they are walking the dog – and many young children consider this an exciting treat, even if they usually consider walking to be a boring chore.

HIDE AND SEEK

Traditional games never lose their appeal for young children, and playing something as simple as hide and seek is a great, fun way to get young children moving about. Simply take it in turns to hide and seek, but try to set a short time limit to encourage 'seekers' to run around as fast as possible. You could also think about introducing your child to other playground games such as hopscotch, hula hoop and follow my leader – and don't forget a fast-paced game of chase.

DRESSING UP

It can be challenging to keep children away from the television on rainy days, but a well-stocked dressing-up box should keep your child amused for hours. Try to build up a collection of 'active' costumes – think about superheroes, firemen, pirates, policemen or even your child's favourite pop stars, television or film characters. These don't need to be too elaborate or expensive – often a plastic policeman's helmet or fireman's hat will be enough to set the ball rolling. Animal costumes are also a good option. Helping your child to dress up as a cat – with pipe-cleaner whiskers, cardboard ears and a tail – can encourage them to run and jump about, and a horse's tail can be enough to get them trotting and galloping around the house and garden for hours on end.

INDOOR PLAY AREAS

It can be difficult to find new activities for young children with short attention spans, especially during winter or in wet weather. This is when indoor play areas really come into their own. Most centres are open to children from birth to 12 years, and offer a wide range of activities from climbing frames, slides, trampolines and rides to ball pools and soft play areas for children under four.

Indoor play areas are now so popular that you should have no problem finding one – or several – in your area. They tend to be open all year round and are very popular with children of all ages.

SKATEBOARDING

Skateboarding is a great option for boys and girls. Whether you live in the town or in the country, your child will always be able to find a place to practise, and can happily spend hours learning new moves and tricks.

Skateboarding isn't recommended for children under the age of six – and it's definitely not suitable for under fives – as children of this age often don't have the balance and coordination needed to control a board. Children under the age of ten should still only ride with adult supervision and always in safe areas away from traffic and pedestrians. It's best not to ride in wet weather, as this can make it harder to control the board.

If your child is interested in skateboarding, then buy a good quality board and make sure that it's well maintained. It's very important to make sure that your child wears the appropriate protective clothing as they are likely to fall off their board many times when they are learning, so a helmet, elbow and wrist guards, and knee pads are all essential kit.

Many parks now have designated skateboard areas where your child can practise. They should also be taught how to fall to reduce the risk of injury and should always build up to new tricks gradually, without trying anything outside of their ability.

Provided all these guidelines are followed, skateboarding can be an exciting hobby for your child that can keep them happy into their teens and beyond. Your local skate shop should be able to help you find the right equipment for your child and give you all the help you need to get started.

GO-KARTING

Go-karting involves driving a low, open-wheeled vehicle around a track or circuit. Unlike a normal car, go-karts sit very close to the ground and are completely open, with no front, back, sides or roof. Although this doesn't give much protection in the event of an accident, the risk of injury is actually minimal. This is because go-karts have a low centre of gravity, which means they are more likely to spin rather than flip over if the driver loses control.

Go-karts are easy to drive as they usually have just two pedals – an accelerator and a brake. Participants are given a full safety briefing before they are allowed to get into their go-kart and are also given a few minutes to get the hang of it before they are allowed onto the track with other drivers.

Go-karting is suitable for children over the age of eight, and is often considered to be the best way into motor sports and Formula 1 – world champions Nigel Mansell, Alain Prost, Ayrton Senna and Michael Schumacher were all successful kart racers, so was Lewis Hamilton – so it's the perfect choice if your child is interested in cars or motor racing.

If you think your child might be interested in more than an occasional race around the track, then it's a good idea to look into go-karting classes. Comer Cadet and WTP Cadet classes are designed for children aged eight to twelve years old and are recognized by the Motor Sports Association (MSA), which is the governing body for go-karting. Some of these have a minimum weight restriction, which means that your child needs to be a certain weight to take part in the class. If you think your child would like to compete, the MSA can help you to find a recognized club in your area.

WATER SPORTS

Young children can enjoy sailing with their families, but those aged eight and over can learn to sail a boat by themselves. Onboard is a new initiative from the Royal Yachting Association (RYA) designed to introduce sailing and windsurfing to children aged eight and over. Over the next ten years, Onboard aims to work with clubs across the UK to introduce half a million children to these sports. You don't even need to live near the sea to take part, as you can learn on lakes, estuaries and rivers too.

Part of the appeal of sailing lessons is that children get a very hands-on experience. Children usually go out in a boat on their own or with one friend, but they will always sail as part of a group, so an instructor is always nearby in case they need help. As buoyancy aids are worn at all times, it doesn't even matter if your child can't swim, although it does help if they are confident in the water as they are likely to get wet or fall in, particularly if they are windsurfing. Although your child can wear normal outdoor clothes for sailing, they will need to wear a wetsuit for windsurfing lessons. Your local sailing club should have plenty of these available for hire, so you don't need to worry about having all the right gear.

Confident swimmers could also have a go at surfing. Surf schools tend to set their own age restrictions, but most take children from around the age of six to eight. Many surf schools run classes specially designed for children – and some are designed so that the whole family can learn together. At the beginning of each class, the instructor will run through the basic techniques on the beach, before taking to the water to practise.

Water-skiing and wakeboarding are also options for children aged eight and over. Water-skiing involves being pulled along behind a motorboat while standing upright on two water-skis. Wakeboarding combines elements of water-skiing, snowboarding and surfing and is a bit like water-skiing on a small surfboard instead of skis. Cable wakeboard, where the rider is pulled along by an overheard cable rather than a boat, is also increasingly popular. Wakeboarding tends to be more popular with children as it's easier to learn, but most centres insist that children can swim at least 50 metres, and minimum age limits do vary.

In recent years, scuba diving has also become available to children as young as eight. The PADI Bubblemaker programme is a one-off session that teaches children how to dive in a swimming pool to a depth of two metres, using full scuba equipment. Participants swim and play under water, and learn the basics of scuba diving.

After the Bubblemaker session, children can move on to the Seal Team Program. This is available to children aged between eight and twelve years old, and also takes place in a swimming pool. The first part of the course challenges children to complete five levels, which cover basic safety techniques and scuba diving skills. Once they have done this, they become a PADI Seal Team Member and are awarded the PADI Seal Certificate. They can then go on to attempt 'Speciality Aquamissions', which include learning about wreck diving, night diving and environmental awareness. When they have completed nine specialty missions they then become a PADI Master Seal Team member.

All equipment is provided and sessions last between 60 and 90 minutes – and as Seal Team is an ongoing course, it can keep your child busy for months.

You could also think about introducing your child to canoeing or kayaking. There are three basic types of canoe:

▶ *A kayak is a closed cockpit boat in which the paddler sits and uses a double-ended paddle.*
▶ *A canoe is very similar to a kayak except the paddler kneels and uses a single-ended paddle.*
▶ *An open canoe is an open boat, which is usually larger than a kayak. Paddlers (there is usually more than one) kneel and used single-ended paddles.*

You can choose to paddle on calm waters or rapids and there are a variety of disciplines within canoeing, including slalom and sprint. Clubs will usually have all the equipment available for you to borrow. Most clubs will expect your child to be able to swim 50 metres, and there is often a minimum age limit of nine years. In some areas you can even learn the basics in a swimming pool. Contact the British Canoe Union (BCU) to find a club in your area.

SKIING AND SNOWBOARDING

If you enjoy skiing, then why not ask your child if they would like to give it a go? Most dry ski slopes offer skiing and snowboarding lessons plus a range of other activities for children aged five and over – and some offer one-to-one skiing lessons for children as young as three. Sno Tubing – where children sit inside inflatable rings – and Sno Bobbing – which is similar to sledging – are also great fun for children aged four and over, and don't require your child to learn any new skills.

Older children are more likely to be interested in snowboarding than skiing, as it has a much cooler reputation. Although children as young as three can be taught to ski, snowboarding should be started a few years later – at around age five to seven – as it requires more muscle strength and coordination. Lessons are essential and it's important to make sure that all equipment fits properly. For this reason many parents opt to buy rather than rent, although this can be a waste of money if your child is only likely to use them a few times before they grow out of them.

If your child gets the hang of it and is keen to try skiing on real snow, you could always consider a family skiing holiday. Most resorts offer dedicated children's programmes and group lessons, and all equipment is usually available to hire. You will find more information on family ski holidays later in this chapter.

Snowboarding safety

Snowboarding has a slightly higher risk of injury than skiing, so it's important to take lessons and use the recommended safety equipment. Most injuries are to the wrists, and wearing wrist guards can cut the risk of injury by as much as half. Head injuries are also fairly common, so your child should always wear a helmet to protect them if they fall. You can also reduce the risk of ankle injury by making sure that your child wears boots that are not too soft, to give the ankle some support.

The Scout and Guide Association

One of the most effective ways to introduce children to a range of sports and activities is to enrol them in the Scout or Guide

Association. Both organizations were founded by Sir Robert Baden Powell in the early 1900s, with the intention of creating a 'training scheme' for young people that would prepare them for adult life.

In recent years, the Scouts and the Guides have worked hard to shed their stuffy image, and have enjoyed continued popularity as a result. They cater for children from the age of five – with senior members up to the age of 18 – and offer an impressive range of events and activities. All groups have their own uniform and leaders work hard to bring out the best in each and every child.

THE SCOUT ASSOCIATION

Although the Scouts were once open only to boys, this has changed and roughly 10 per cent of members are now female. The Scout movement was designed to help children learn new skills and grow in confidence, while having fun and making new friends. The scouts are made up of four groups, each catering for a different age group with a variety of age-appropriate activities on offer.

▶ **Beaver Scouts**
The Beavers are aged between six and eight and meet in groups known as 'colonies'. Popular activities include arts and crafts, and going on trips to various places of interest.

▶ **Cub Scouts**
Cubs are between the ages of eight and ten and meet in 'packs', which are split into smaller groups called 'sixes'. Children of this age are treated to camping trips and day trips along with a range of creative pastimes.

▶ **Scouts**
Between the ages of ten and fourteen, children can join the Scouts. Scouts are organized into 'troops' of ten, and often

take part in a range of challenge award schemes, which include activities such as abseiling, camping and swimming.

▶ **Explorer Scouts**
From the age of 14 to 18, young people may join the Explorer Scouts and take part in the Duke of Edinburgh's Award Scheme and the Queen's Scout's Award. Many members go on to become Scout Leaders themselves.

THE GUIDE ASSOCIATION

Like the Scouts, the Girl Guides is also split into four sections, each of which caters for a different age group.

▶ **Rainbows**
Any girl aged five to seven can become a Rainbow. This is the youngest of the Girl Guide groups, and focuses on a range of activities known as the 'Rainbow Jigsaw'. Activities include games and creative hobbies, visiting people and places of interest and occasional overnight sleepover events.

▶ **Brownies**
Girls aged seven to ten can join the Brownies. A group of Brownies is known as a 'pack', and is split into small groups called 'sixes'. They meet regularly and are given lots of opportunities to take part in a range of events and activities throughout the year. These include games and sports, physical challenges, sleepovers and camps.

▶ **Guides**
The Guides is open to girls aged ten to fourteen. Guides work together in 'patrols', elect their own leader and are encouraged to plan their own activities. The Guide programme is very diverse, and patrols learn about subjects including physical and emotional wellbeing, global awareness and interpersonal and life skills. They are also are encouraged to take part in a range of creative and adventurous activities.

► **The Senior Section**
The Senior Section is open to young women aged 14 to 18 and is linked to a variety of recognized qualifications and awards, including the Duke of Edinburgh's Award Scheme.

Brownies and Guides

Tiffany joined the Brownies when she was eight. The group meets at my daughter's school and is very popular, so there was a waiting list of almost a year. It only costs £1 each week, so is an inexpensive way to keep her busy. In Brownies, Tiffany did a mixture of games, crafts, parties, walks and other events like fun days, sleepovers and camps.

When she turned ten, Tiffany joined the Guides, which is similar to Brownies but a bit more grown-up. It's been good for her to mix with older girls, but she was a bit nervous about it until I started helping out on a volunteer basis. I help out with games and activities, talk to the girls and generally have fun with them. Brownies and Guides have been good for Tiffany. She's learned lots of new skills, made new friends and her confidence has improved. I enjoy it too.

Jo is mum to Tiffany, 11.

Active holidays

A family holiday is the perfect opportunity to show your child that keeping fit and active can be lots of fun. Without the distraction of friends, television, computer games and long telephone conversations, you should find it easier to motivate your child to get active. Even a traditional beach holiday can be surprisingly active – there's a good chance that your child will be in and out of the pool or the sea all day, and walking and running about in the sand, or even building sandcastles, can significantly increase the amount of exercise they get each day.

If you're serious about getting active as a family – and suspect that a beach holiday means that you're likely to spend a week or two lying on a sunlounger – then you could always consider booking an active holiday instead. There are plenty of options, so you should be able to find something that is suitable for your family.

CYCLING HOLIDAYS

Cycling holidays operate all over the world and although you can choose to go it alone and plan your own trip, you will undoubtedly find it easier to book a trip through a specialist travel company. This has several important benefits: the travel company organizes your accommodation, plans your route, transports your bikes and usually transfers your luggage from location to location, leaving you to enjoy the scenery at your own pace.

It can be tricky to take children between the ages of four and eight on cycling holidays, as they are too old to sit in a child seat or trailer, but too young to cycle for long distances by themselves. That's not to say that this sort of holiday won't work for you, but it might be best to opt for a single-centre holiday, where you venture out on a planned bike ride each day, and return to the same place. That way you can tailor each ride to your child's age and ability. It's important always to ride at the pace of the slowest rider and make regular stops, particularly if you have young children – so don't expect to cover great distances and be prepared to take your time.

HORSE RIDING HOLIDAYS

If your child has shown an interest in horse riding, you could think about a riding holiday. Trekking holidays can be a great way to see some beautiful scenery and escape from the hustle and bustle of everyday life, but they can be surprisingly hard work for inexperienced riders. Instead, you might prefer to look for an instructional holiday, where the whole family can learn how to improve their riding skills. It's best to have a few lessons at home first though, just to make sure that everyone is happy on horseback.

CLUB HOLIDAYS

If you don't want to stray too far from a traditional holiday format but want to make sure there are lots of activities on offer, then a sports resort such as Club La Santa or Club La Manga could be perfect. These offer plenty of dedicated children's activities, along with a range of sports to keep everyone active. Family holiday specialists such as Mark Warner and Nielson are also great options for families with young children, and holiday centres such as Center Parcs also offer mini-breaks and holidays in the UK and Europe with a strong focus on sport, fitness and fun. You could also consider traditional British holiday companies such as Butlins and Pontins, which offer an impressive range of reasonably priced activities, including go-karting, quad biking, archery and snorkelling. So you should be able to find something that pleases everyone, even if you're on a budget.

ADVENTURE HOLIDAYS

If your child is aged seven or over, they might enjoy an adventure holiday with a company such as PGL. Although holidays for families are also available, the company is best known for organizing activity holidays for unaccompanied children. These take place at various locations in the UK and France and cover a diverse range of outdoor pursuits from pony trekking, motorbiking, swimming and water sports to more familiar activities such as football and dance. This kind of holiday is a great way for your child to learn new activities and make new friends, and spending time away from home can help to create a sense of independence and boost their confidence no end.

WATER SPORTS

If water sports appeal to your child, you could think about a sailing, cruise or canal boat holiday. These don't involve intense bursts of activity, but do encourage your child to enjoy spending time outdoors. If you think that your child would enjoy trying out a range of water sports, then look for a specialist centre such as Plas Menai in North Wales. This offers a variety of adventure breaks, suitable for families with children aged eight and over. You can have a go at a range of water sports including dinghy sailing and water-skiing – and if your child finds a sport that they enjoy, there's plenty of advice on how to progress and gain proficiency awards and certificates.

SKIING AND SNOWBOARDING

In winter you could opt for a family skiing holiday. Many companies cater for very young children, so even if they are too young to ski or snowboard, they will be able to play in the snow in child-friendly areas – and building a snowman or having a snowball fight can be great exercise. Many of the big tour operators offer family-oriented breaks, or you could try family specialists such as Mark Warner, Ski Famille or Ski Esprit.

CAMPING

Most children love the idea of a camping trip, but parents can understandably find the idea quite daunting. Although it takes a little planning and preparation, a camping trip is the perfect way to encourage a love of the outdoors – and it's virtually impossible not to be active in the process.

Many campsites now have modern facilities, so there's no need to worry about being without a shower or a flushing toilet. Camping is also a significantly cheaper way to have a family holiday, and if you venture to sunnier climes, you don't even have to worry about getting rained on.

If you have never been camping before, or have never done it with a child in tow, have a practice run by pitching a tent in your garden and sleeping out there for the night. Your child will probably love the experience, so if it's a success the next step is an overnight or weekend trip.

Many farms have specially designated areas for camping, which is a perfect way for young children to spend time in the country and see lots of farm animals. You could also consider heading for the coast, so that your child can play on the beach – which is an exciting treat even in bad weather. Cooking, collecting firewood and fetching water are important aspects of the camping experience – and you can get your child actively involved in every one of them.

If you are planning to go on long walks or hikes, then make sure you travel light and don't expect children to walk more than one mile for each year in age. So, for example, you could aim to cover seven miles per day with a seven-year-old, but only three miles with a three-year-old – and you will probably find that to be an ambitious goal.

If you don't own a tent, or don't want to spend time too far away from civilization, look for an organized campsite where you can hire luxury tents that are already pitched. Many of these even have electric lights and their own kitchens – or you could opt for a caravan or mobile home instead. Campsites of this type often have plenty of organized children's activities, restaurants and swimming pools, which may work better if you have young children or are planning to stay for a week or more.

Before you go camping, bear in mind the Boy Scout motto: Be prepared. If you are taking your own tent, check that you know how to put it up, and make sure that the whole family have warm and waterproof clothing in case of bad weather. It's a good idea to give everyone their own torch to use at night, and make sure that children know how to find the way back to your tent just in case you get separated.

Above all, keep the focus firmly on having fun and spending time together as a family. Away from the distractions of television and computer games you will be surprised how much more active your child becomes.

Sports camps

Sports camps are a great way to keep your child active during the school holidays. They have long been popular with American families, and are now increasingly popular in the UK. Some camps are residential, but day camps tend to be the most popular choice for parents of younger children. These operate to the same hours as the typical school day, which can also solve problems with childcare. Most camps are open to school-age children – five is usually the minimum age – and cater for all interests, from art and music to sport and dance. However, the majority of camps have a strong emphasis on sports and activities, and some specialize in just one area such as football or cricket.

There are so many summer camps available that it can be hard to know which one is best for your child. But unless your child has a particular interest or ability in one area, you might find it's best to opt for a traditional summer camp experience, which gives them the chance to try out lots of different activities.

Before you commit, it's important to make sure that the camp is licensed and fully registered with a governing body. It's worth checking the ratio of instructors to campers and campers to equipment, to ensure that your child will get plenty of supervision and lots of opportunity to try a variety of activities. You should also consider any hidden costs, such as transport, lunch money and pocket money.

Once you have identified a camp that seems suitable, it's wise to take your child for a visit or attend an open day. It's not worth making a booking unless you and your child are happy, or else you may find that your child is begging to come home on their first day. Take the time to talk to staff, and make sure that facilities are well maintained and seem clean and safe. Remember to ask your child what they think, as it's not a good idea to push them into it if they seem at all unsure. If you or your child is nervous about committing to an entire week, many camps offer one-day, three-day or morning sessions, which can be perfect for the less confident child. Whatever you decide, it's wise to book early, especially if you have more than one child, as places are usually limited.

> **Insight**
>
> Don't book a sporting/activity holiday unless your family is already fairly active. Instead, think about planning a few walks, beach games or even crazy golf into your usual holiday routine. Aim for just one activity a day, and the whole family will go home fitter than when you arrived.

TEST YOUR KNOWLEDGE

1 At what age can children start basic dance/movement classes?

2 From what age is it safe for your child to start skateboarding?

3 Does your child need to be a confident swimmer before they can have sailing lessons?

4 What is wakeboarding?

5 From what age can children learn to scuba dive?

6 At what age can your child start having skiing lessons?

7 Can girls join the Scouts?

8 What are the Beavers?

9 What are the Rainbows?

10 From what age can your child go on an adventure holiday?

....

Answers

1 From 18 months
2 Six
3 No, buoyancy aids are worn at all times, so even non-swimmers can take part.
4 Water-skiing on a small surfboard rather than skis
5 From eight years
6 In some areas lessons are available to children as young as three.

7 Yes, girls make up around 10 per cent of members.
8 Scouts aged six to eight
9 Girl Guides aged five to seven
10 Unaccompanied children aged seven and over can go on adventure holidays with companies such as PGL.

6

School sports

In this chapter you will learn:
- *why PE is an important part of your child's curriculum*
- *how to improve your child's skills*
- *why your child could benefit from joining an after-school sports club.*

Most parents show a keen interest in the academic aspects of their child's education and routinely ask what their child is studying, encourage them to work hard and make sure that homework gets done. Unfortunately, parents rarely show the same level of interest in their child's physical education (PE), even though it is an important part of the school curriculum.

A core subject for life

Some parents overlook their child's performance in PE lessons because they assume that it's not very important and has no real bearing on their child's future. But this couldn't be further from the truth. Just as a child's ability in academic subjects such as English and maths can determine their performance in exams and their potential to succeed in a chosen career, so can their participation in PE lessons improve their long-term health and happiness. What's more, children who don't do well in PE often develop a negative attitude towards sport and exercise which can last for the rest of their lives, so it's important to show your support and encourage your child to do their best.

Many parents don't realize that PE teaches children much more than how to throw or catch a ball. It helps them to develop important life skills – and can even improve their academic performance. In fact, some specialist sports colleges have proved that a focus on learning through sports can help children do better in the classroom. And that's not the only benefit. Taking part in sports and PE can help your child in the following ways:

- ▶ *It can teach your child about the importance of teamwork.*
- ▶ *Tactical sports can improve your child's problem-solving abilities.*
- ▶ *It can teach your child how to make effective decisions.*
- ▶ *It can help your child to develop self-confidence.*
- ▶ *It can reveal your child's natural leadership qualities.*
- ▶ *It teaches your child how to deal with success and failure.*
- ▶ *Throwing and catching can improve coordination and help develop the hand movements used in writing.*
- ▶ *Taking part in early-morning activities can help improve your child's concentration throughout the day.*
- ▶ *Children are less disruptive after taking part in PE classes or lunchtime activities.*

For these reasons it's vital to encourage your child to work just as hard at PE as they would in academic subjects, so don't write notes to excuse them unless there is a very good reason, no matter how persuasive they are. If you don't already know, make an effort to find out about the sports provision at your child's school. Check what's on offer, find out about after-school clubs – and encourage your child to get involved.

Did you know?
In terms of exam results, sports colleges are improving at a faster rate than all other specialist schools. The share of pupils getting more than five good GCSE passes has increased from 49 per cent in 2005 to 56 per cent in 2006. So PE really can help children learn.

PE provision in schools

How much PE should my child's school provide? In response to widespread concerns about childhood obesity, the government wants all schools to provide at least two hours of physical activity for pupils each week (including PE lessons, after-school clubs and practice sessions), with the aim to increase this to five hours by 2012. As a result of government funding and school sport partnerships, some schools have stepped up to the challenge. A recent government survey showed that some schools now offer up to 42 different sports – primary schools offer an average of 15, while secondary schools offer an average of 20 – so your child's PE teacher should be able to help your child find something they enjoy.

Insight

PE lessons have changed in recent years, and the focus is now firmly on fun. So push bad memories of being sent on cross-country runs in the snow and rain to the back of your mind and be positive about all the new skills your child is going to learn.

Although school sports have undergone some changes in recent years, traditional sports and activities tend to be the most popular. Government statistics show that sports most commonly played in schools are:

- *football (in 98 per cent of schools)*
- *dance (in 96 per cent of schools)*
- *gymnastics (in 95 per cent of schools)*
- *athletics (in 92 per cent of schools)*
- *cricket (in 89 per cent of schools).*

With the possible exception of dance, these sports have been central to PE lessons for decades – you can probably remember taking part in some of them during your own schooldays, so already have a good idea of the rules and basic skills involved.

As children grow up and progress through the school system, the
structure of their PE lessons and the types of activities on offer will
change. At first your child will concentrate on basic skills such as
throwing, catching, running and jumping, before progressing to
team games and other activities. It's a good idea to practise these
basic skills with your child even before they start school, as they
form the foundation of their physical education and will help to
build their confidence and increase motivation.

The National Curriculum

The Natural Curriculum was introduced to state schools in England,
Wales and Northern Ireland in 1988. It sets out exactly what the
government decides children should be learning throughout their
school career, and gives performance targets according to your
child's age. It covers PE as well as academic subjects, and is designed
to ensure that all children at state schools cover the same basic
material throughout their education, irrespective of their individual
abilities.

When it comes to PE, schools have a great deal of flexibility in terms
of how they teach the skills set out in the National Curriculum. This
means that schools can, within reason, decide which sports and
activities to teach, although this decision is usually influenced by the
facilities available and the expertise of the teachers.

The National Curriculum is broken down into three sections, or Key Stages, and assessments are carried out at the end of each stage. These are known as Key Stage 1 (for children aged five to seven), Key Stage 2 (for children aged seven to eleven) and Key Stage 3 (for children aged 11 to 14). After this, children are allowed to opt in or out of some subjects, and their performance is measured by coursework and their GCSEs and/or other vocational qualifications.

Children are expected to develop particular skills in each of these Key Stages, across a variety of disciplines. You can help them achieve these goals by practising at home as often as you can.

Key Stage 1

Key Stage 1 is the official terminology for the first two years of your child's school career in England and Wales. This is the first stage of primary education, also known as Year 1 and Year 2, and covers the period when pupils are between five and seven years old.

CONTENT: BASIC LEVEL

During this stage of their education, your child will be introduced to a variety of activities at a basic level. The National Curriculum requires that children of this age should receive tuition in dance, games, gymnastics and, ideally, swimming. These activities build a solid foundation from which your child can go on to learn the skills required to play specific sports.

Dance
Through dance, your child will learn good movement skills and improve balance, coordination and flexibility. They will be encouraged to use their imagination and creativity – perhaps by moving like an animal or growing like a flower – and will be taught simple dances and be expected to perform them to the class.

Insight

Don't assume that dancing is just for girls. Many boys enjoy dancing too, and it's a great way for them to build confidence and improve their balance. So don't tease boys if they show an interest in dance – you could have the next Billy Elliott on your hands.

Games

This will help to develop your child's game-playing skills, particularly throwing and catching. They will be introduced to simple net games such as tennis and badminton, and also striking and fielding games such as rounders and cricket. In these activities, children are taught how to use skills, tactics and strategies to outwit the opposition and will provide the opportunity to play in small competitive teams.

Gymnastics

Gymnastics helps to teach your child how to control their movements and improve their balance and agility. They will be taught to perform basic moves on the floor, such as jumps and rolls, and will be shown how to copy short sequences of movements. Once they have got the hang of this, they will be shown how to perform these using apparatus.

Swimming

It's not compulsory for schools to teach swimming to children of this age, but many schools do. Initially children are encouraged to enjoy being in the water, and move and float using buoyancy aids. They will be taught how to move their arms and legs and perform basic strokes with a view to learning how to swim. Once they have learned how to swim, they will be able to take part in a range of other water-based activities.

HOW TO HELP AND SUPPORT YOUR CHILD IN KEY STAGE 1

At this stage, your child should be having lots of fun in their PE lessons. They are unlikely to be introduced to competitive sports until Key Stage 2 – and even then on a very limited basis – so the focus should be on learning how to use and control their bodies.

Without realizing it, it's likely that you are already helping your child to develop and refine these skills. In a typical trip to the park or playground most of the games your child plays will probably involve running, jumping, climbing and balancing. For example, climbing the steps up to the slide, walking across a low balance bar or jumping off the climbing frame are essentially the same skills that your child will be taught in gymnastics. Similarly, running after a ball, kicking, throwing and catching are all skills that your child will be helped to develop in games.

It's a good idea to encourage your child to take part in all of these playground activities, but there are several more straightforward, but very effective, ways in which you can help your child to improve their performance.

Running
Running is the basis of several sports, so it's a good idea to encourage your child to run as much as possible. It's best to do this in the garden or the park, so they won't hurt themselves if they fall, but any safe area away from traffic or other hazards is fine too. Children usually respond best if you give them an obvious target to aim for, so challenging them to a race to the next tree in the park or the playground swings should motivate them to get moving.

Children are usually more enthusiastic if you run with them, but try to maintain a roughly similar pace, as they will quickly lose interest if you run off into the distance at top speed – and this won't help to build their confidence either. Improve their skills by asking them to swerve around objects, and be sure to teach younger children how to stop effectively. The best way to demonstrate this is to show them to transfer their weight to the front foot, which then acts as a brake.

Throwing and catching
Throwing and catching are important skills to master before your child is introduced to fielding games such as rounders and cricket. Most children love ball games, so all you need is a small- to medium-sized soft, light ball that fits easily into your child's hands.

Begin by teaching your child to throw underarm. The best way to do this is to show them how to throw the ball a little way up into the air and make a cup shape with their hands to catch it. Once they have got the hang of this, you can then start playing games of catch. Start quite close together, and gradually move further apart as their skills improve.

Once your child has mastered this, you can move on to overarm throwing. It's best to practise against a wall, so that your child has an easy target to hit – and when the ball bounces back to them they can practise their catching skills too. If your child is right-handed, teach them to put their left foot forward when they throw, and vice versa. They should also be taught to look at the target as they throw, to help improve their aim.

Catching also requires practice. Many children find this a more difficult skill to master, as it requires a certain amount of hand–eye coordination. Teach your child to make a target with their hands so that the person throwing knows where to aim, and then watch the flight of the ball so that they can make sure they are in the right position to catch it. They will be less likely to miss or drop the ball if they cup their hands ready to receive it, then fold their fingers around it and move their hands in towards their body as they catch.

Challenge your child to catch the ball a certain number of times during a game of catch, and try to improve your score with every game. Then try to throw and catch faster and faster and over greater distances to improve their aim and accuracy.

Batting
Rounders and cricket are usually the first fielding games that your child will be taught to play, so your child will need to learn how to hit the ball. Encourage them to practise in the garden, park – or even on the beach – with a small, lightweight bat and tennis ball-sized bouncy ball.

Until your child gets the hang of it, it's important to bowl slowly and make the ball bounce at least once before it reaches your child.

Teach them to stand sideways and hold the bat firmly, taking a very short swing before they hit. Give them lots of encouragement, and be sure to cheer when they hit the ball. When they have mastered this, challenge them to see how many times in a row they can strike the ball – and then teach them how to swing the bat harder so that they can hit the ball greater distances.

Insight

Look out for lightweight bats that are covered with Velcro – these are usually sold with soft fabric balls that stick to the Velcro pads. Practising with these is great way to help your child improve their hand–eye coordination and teach them how to make contact between bat and ball – something that young children often struggle with.

Kicking

Most children find it quite easy to kick a ball, but with a little practice you can help them to improve their accuracy and learn how to kick over greater distances. Show your child how to keep the non-kicking foot alongside the ball and keep their head over the ball as they kick. When they need to kick short distances or dribble the ball, they should kick with the side of their foot, and kick with the top of the foot when they want the ball to travel longer distances or have more power. They will find it easier to improve their aim if they have a target, so help them to build a goal, or chalk up a target on a wall instead. Give your child lots of opportunity to improve their aim before you start playing with a goalkeeper.

Balancing

It's very important to help develop your child's sense of balance as this will improve their abilities in a range of activities from running, catching and throwing to athletics, dance and gymnastics. Begin by challenging your child to stand on one leg and encourage them to balance for as long as they can – then do the same with the other leg. Once they have mastered this, encourage them to hop on one leg for as long as they can. Another good exercise is to ask your child to walk along a line drawn on the ground, or balance along a low wall or on playground stepping stones. You could even set up your own assault courses and challenge your child to complete these exercises as fast as they can.

Swimming

Until your child has learned how to swim, it's a good idea to take them to the swimming pool every week to help build their confidence in water. Most children enjoy splashing around, so focus on having fun and gradually introduce them to the basic arm and leg movements they will need to move themselves through the water. If your child is nervous in the water, you may find it's helpful to enrol them in private swimming lessons. Other parents find that a family holiday is the perfect opportunity to turn their child into a water baby. Going swimming and playing in the water every day, particularly outdoors when the sun is shining, can often help even the most nervous swimmer to learn how to enjoy the water.

Insight

If you're a nervous swimmer, it's tempting to leave it up to your school to teach your child to swim. However, your child will progress much more quickly if you take them swimming on a regular basis. Aim to go at least once each month – ideally once per week – and you might find that you become more confident in the water too.

Key Stage 2

Key Stage 2 is the second, and final, part of your child's primary education and covers a period of four years, otherwise known as Years 3 to 6.

CONTENT: PROGRESSION AND SUPPLEMENTARY ACTIVITIES

When your child graduates to Key Stage 2 (which covers ages seven to eleven) they will be encouraged to develop their existing skills and take part in a range of new activities. Dance, games and gymnastics are still compulsory at this stage, but your child's school can select two further activities from the following: athletics, swimming and outdoor and adventurous activities.

Dance
In Key Stage 2 children are encouraged to use dance to communicate a range of ideas and issues, along with their own thoughts and feelings. They will also be taught about the historical and cultural significance of dance and will be expected to create short dances of their own and perform them to the class.

Games
Now that they have been taught the basics, children are expected to improve their skills and play simple net, striking/fielding and invasion games with other children, as part of a team. Teaching will focus on developing skills and tactics, defending, attacking and outwitting the opposition.

Gymnastics
In Key Stage 2, children will be encouraged to increase their range of basic gymnastic skills. They will also be expected to create sequences of different movements, using both the floor and the apparatus.

Swimming
Ideally, most children should have learned to swim by this stage – so the focus is on swimming increasing distances unaided, and at greater speeds, and performing a variety of strokes. Children will also be taught water safety and survival skills.

Athletics
Most children are introduced to athletics halfway through Year 3. Lessons will focus on running, jumping and throwing skills and they will be expected to steadily improve their speed and stamina. They will compete against other children in simple competitions.

Outdoor and adventurous activities
In outdoor and adventurous activities children learn to follow maps and trails and try to solve physical problems and challenges.

Working on their own or in small groups, they will take part in simple orientation exercises using maps and diagrams.

HOW TO HELP AND SUPPORT YOUR CHILD IN KEY STAGE 2

During Key Stage, 2 the emphasis is on increasing your child's creativity and independence. During this time they will be exposed to a wider variety of games and activities and given the opportunity to learn new skills. Children of this age are putting all their basic skills together and using them to play competitive games. Many children enjoy this, but you may find that if your child is less able, they become reluctant to compete. Help them to overcome this by taking as much time as you can to practise with them, giving them lots of opportunity to show you their new skills and being interested in and enthusiastic about every achievement.

Dance

Encourage your child by exposing them to as many different types of music as possible. If they enjoy dance, you could think about offering them private lessons, or if that isn't an option, encourage them to practise outside of school with friends and put on a show.

Games

Take the time to play a range of simple games with your child. Encourage your child to use as many skills as possible – for example, batting, catching and running – and invite friends for a game of rounders in the park. If your child isn't confident about their abilities, continue to work on their basic skills such as catching, batting or throwing, until their confidence improves.

Gymnastics

If you have a garden, encourage your child to practise handstands, cartwheels and forward rolls on the grass, to increase their balance and flexibility. Indoor play areas often have plenty of climbing frames and equipment that encourage children to jump, climb and balance, so consider making regular visits so that your child can practise.

Swimming

If your child has not learned how to swim by Year 4, and is still nervous in the water, you may want to think about enrolling them in some private swimming lessons. This can often give children the extra attention and encouragement they need to start swimming. If your child is particularly scared of the water, you may find that they feel better if you are in the water with them so make weekly swimming sessions a priority and use flotation devices such as armbands to build your child's confidence. As their skills improve, gradually reduce the amount of air in their armbands so that they learn how to support themselves in the water, without worrying that they are going to sink.

Athletics

Once your child has been introduced to athletics, it's a good idea to set them increasingly difficult challenges to help them refine their skills. As in Key Stage 1, encourage them to run as fast as they can or over greater distances – a relay race or even a game of tag can help with this. Help them to practise jumping by seeing how high or how far they can jump, and challenging them to improve their performance every time. The focus here is on steady improvement – so reinforce the idea that they can get better and better results with practice.

Insight

Help your child to understand that practice makes perfect. The understanding that they have to put in time and effort if they want to be good at something will serve them well both at school and in their later career. So encourage their efforts and help them to celebrate every achievement.

Outdoor and adventurous activities

If your child is taking part in orienteering, the best way to help is to walk as a family every weekend. If you live near a woodland area or nature trail, ask you child to help guide you around your chosen route. Alternatively, draw up a basic map and ask your child to help you find your way through an unfamiliar environment. On a smaller scale, activities such as treasure hunts, which help to improve their problem-solving abilities, can also be a great way to encourage them and have fun at the same time.

Key Stage 3 and beyond

At age 11 children begin their secondary education and move to a new school. At this point they begin Key Stage 3 (which covers children aged 11 to 14) and will be entering Year 7.

CONTENT: TEAMWORK AND COMPETITION

Children of this age will have been taught all the basic skills needed for them to play sports competitively, and will now be expected to play as part of a team and compete against their classmates. They will gradually be encouraged to try out different roles and responsibilities. For instance, they may begin to specialize in a particular sport or sports, start to play in a particular position, and, as they progress in their secondary education, they might compete in tournaments or even become a team captain.

At this stage, PE lessons usually become much more flexible and children usually have many more sports and activities to choose from. There is a good reason for this. Research has shown that pre-teens are increasingly likely to drop out of sports in favour of other, more sedentary, hobbies and pastimes, so it's vital to keep them interested as they grow from children to teenagers. There are various reasons why children of this age lose interest in sports, but the most common ones are that their interests change, they feel under too much pressure to perform, they aren't performing well or they no longer have enough time to devote to sports practice. It's also important to recognize that many young people feel self-conscious about their changing bodies as they go through puberty and may be reluctant to put themselves in any position – including the gym changing rooms – where they could be teased or ridiculed.

If you notice that your child is losing enthusiasm for sport, then take some time to talk to them and find out why. If they really have lost interest, then there is nothing to be gained by forcing them to continue with a sport. Research has shown that girls are more likely than boys to lose interest in sport, but the GirlsActive initiative has found that girls would be much more willing to participate if they were offered alternative forms of activity such as boxercise, street dance and trampolining.

Fortunately, many schools have started to offer a wider range of activities to combat this problem, although children are still required to take part in competitive sports until Year 10. From then on, they can opt out altogether and choose from a range of other activities – so find out what's on offer at your child's school and talk about the options together. It's very important to help your child find something else that appeals as, at this stage, it's all too easy to give up sport altogether. It may take time, but encourage your child to try out a range of activities until they find something else they enjoy.

Competitive sports

Schools have to teach competitive games and activities to children in Key Stages 1 to 3. This means that children begin to play competitively, on a very small scale, when they are five years old, and continue until they can opt out in Year 10, at age 14 or 15.

It's important to remember that schools have to cater for all levels of sporting ability. Some children are natural athletes and may go on to represent their school, their county, or even their country. Others are less able, or may have health concerns or disabilities that affect their performance. Some parents worry that competitive sports can be unfair on less able children and serve only to teach them that they are not good enough to take part. Certainly, being put in a position where they repeatedly fail is not good for a child's confidence – particularly if they are teased or humiliated by other children who feel that their poor performance is letting the side down.

··

Insight

If your child struggles in PE lessons, have a word with their teacher. Not all children will excel, and those that don't shouldn't be teased or made to feel embarrassed if they can't keep up. Work with your child's teacher to identify an activity that they can enjoy, before they decide that they 'hate' sport and stop trying.

··

However, when managed correctly, studies show that competition can be good for children, whatever their ability. Experts claim that healthy competition motivates children to succeed, refines their skills and encourages them to try harder. Competition doesn't have to be at a high level to get the best out of your child. In fact low-level competition is often better for your child, particularly if they have only just started playing sports. Ideally your child should compete against children of the same age and ability, which is why many schools and clubs have an A, B and C or 1st, 2nd and 3rd team, as well as a novices' team for complete beginners. This not only gives very able children the opportunity to excel, but it also gives less able children a chance to discover how it feels to win – which can greatly increase their confidence.

The government is in the process of developing a school sport national competition framework to increase the amount of competitive opportunities for children and encourage inter-school competitions. The basic framework for competitive sports in schools is already in place and works as follows:

▶ *During Key Stages 1 and 2 children will take part in fun festivals, which allow them to showcase their emerging skills.*
▶ *During Key Stage 2 children will begin to take part in sports competitions.*
▶ *During Key Stages 3 and 4 children will be given access to inter-school leagues and competitions.*

- *Particularly talented athletes may then compete in the UK School Games.*
- *From here a few may progress to playing at county, regional or national level.*

If your child seems unhappy about taking part in competitive sports, you need to find out why. Children who are very able tend to enjoy this kind of activity, so your child probably feels demoralized by their performance or is under too much pressure to perform. Young children in particular need friendly competition, so check that your child's teacher isn't putting too much emphasis on winning or encouraging fierce competition. If this is the case, then it's a good idea to raise the issue with your child's teacher or coach. This kind of environment only helps the most talented athletes and can have disastrous consequences for children who need more support and encouragement.

School sports in the US

There are many similarities between the ways in which school sports are taught in the UK and the US – but there is one important difference. In the UK, PE is part of the National Curriculum, but in the US it is not a part of the core curriculum and there is no national standard, so provision varies greatly not just between states, but also between individual schools.

In order to tackle the obesity problem, US schools are encouraged to provide gym classes five days a week, lasting for one hour per session. But this is not compulsory, and according to the Centers for Disease Control and Prevention, less than 8 per cent of schools actually do this.

As in the UK, PE classes have been cut back in recent years and there is widespread concern that this is, if not contributing to, at least not helping to tackle the issue of childhood obesity. Many PE teachers claim that the No Child Left Behind Act of 2001 (also known as NCLB or 'nickelbee'), which was designed to improve the performance of US primary and secondary schools, is largely responsible for these cutbacks.

Just like the National Curriculum, this legislation requires schools to focus on basic skills such as reading and writing, and developing regular assessments to measure each child's progress as they move through the system. It has caused a great deal of controversy as educational experts argue that it can restrict children's learning, particularly if teachers are only motivated to teach their pupils how to pass regular tests and assessments. PE teachers argue that this has had a particularly negative impact on the provision of physical education. This is because PE is not part of the core curriculum, so it tends to be one of the first classes to be cut back when school administrators need to make budget cuts or free up more time for academic classes.

Following the 2002 Healthy Schools Summit in Washington, DC, the Action for Healthy Kids partnership was formed to address the childhood obesity crisis. This partnership of more than 50 national organizations and government agencies was designed to teach schoolchildren about good nutrition and physical exercise. Schools are now encouraged to sign up to a 'Wellness Program' whereby they commit to encourage healthy eating and provide children from Kindergarten to Grade 12 with daily physical education for the entire school year. After-school clubs and tournaments do not count towards this time. Elementary schools are also expected to provide 20 minutes of supervised recess for active play, and extended periods (two hours or more) of inactivity are discouraged.

Traditionally, PE has been taught in broadly the same way in US schools as it is in the UK. Sports such as American football, baseball, basketball and ice hockey – not to mention cheerleading – take the place of UK stalwarts such as football, rugby and rounders; although the range of sports and activities on offer can vary greatly between schools. Children are usually introduced to simple competitive games in First Grade, when they are six or seven, although many after-school clubs, such as Little League, welcome children from the age of five.

However, this traditional approach to PE lessons is beginning to change. A number of non-profit organizations, such as PE4Life, are now working hard to change the way that PE is taught in the US, with a view to making it more enjoyable and accessible to children of varying abilities. Organizations such as this are encouraging schools to focus on fitness rather than sports. Children are encouraged to run, cycle, dance or climb, while wearing heart rate monitors to ensure that they are working at their target heart rate for the entire class. This approach is designed to teach children about fitness for life and lay the foundation for an active lifestyle, which can continue after they leave formal education. It is particularly beneficial for children who are not natural athletes, as it focuses on setting personal goals and steady improvement, unlike competitive sports, which often don't appeal to the overweight or unfit children who need to exercise the most.

Winning and losing

As soon as your child starts taking part in sport, be positive and encouraging at every step of the way – regardless of their ability or achievements. Try to attend as many matches or sporting events as you can, but give your child the same amount of praise whether they win or lose. Keep the focus on trying their best and steady improvement and resist the temptation to push them too hard, because too much pressure can often be counterproductive.

Case study: How to help a child who struggles with PE

The problem

Laura is an eight-year-old girl who dreads PE lessons because she isn't very sporty. She is a shy child who prefers academic subjects to sports. Although she has some ability in dance and gymnastics, her natural reserve makes it difficult for her to perform confidently in front of her classmates. She has particular problems with ball games, because she isn't confident about throwing, catching or hitting the ball and often misses. Other children make cruel comments about her lack of ability and she is now very reluctant to get involved in any sports for fear of being laughed at.

The solution

Laura's parents, Nicola and Mark, accepted that she was never going to be a sporty child, but didn't want her to be bullied or feel self-conscious. They explained to Laura that she couldn't stop doing PE altogether, but asked what she thought would make her feel better. Laura was keen to improve her skills because this would make her feel more confident, so her parents asked her PE teacher for advice and started to practise basic skills with her every week.

The outcome

Laura didn't mind practising at home as there was no one to judge her or make her feel silly. As a result, her basic skills improved – and so did her confidence. Although Laura will never be a natural athlete, she no longer dreads PE lessons. She is also not as nervous about performing in gymnastics and dance, where she is more able, and her teacher is delighted with her progress.

Extracurricular clubs

Most schools now offer a variety of sport-related breakfast, lunchtime and after-school clubs and activities. Most of these focus on sports and activities that your child will be taught in PE, such as football, gymnastics or hockey, but other, less traditional, activities that don't fit so easily into the curriculum may also be on offer.

Breakfast and after-school clubs can be a blessing for working parents who struggle with childcare issues, but can also be a great way for your child to improve their sporting skills, make new friends and learn in a more relaxed environment where teachers aren't under pressure to follow a pre-planned lesson.

Many of these clubs receive funding from the local authority, but most also rely on help from parents and the wider community. This may involve helping out at clubs on a volunteer basis, or getting involved in fundraising to pay for equipment and teaching staff. Some of these clubs also charge a small weekly fee.

Check with your child's school to find out what after-school clubs are available that might interest your child. And, if you are experienced in a particular sport, perhaps you could offer to help out on a volunteer basis because this makes it easier for schools to keep after-school clubs up and running.

Case study: Making friends through sport

The problem

George is a nine-year-old boy whose parents moved to a new area when he was halfway through Year 5. George has started spending all his free time in front of the television because he has found it hard to settle into his new school and hasn't found it easy to make new friends. Before the move he was very active, and enjoyed riding his bike or playing football with friends, but now he spends all his free time playing computer games and watching television. His parents, Sara and Matt, are worried that he is lonely, but also that he is losing interest in the sports that he used to enjoy.

The solution

Changing schools can be a traumatic experience and George obviously found it hard to adjust. George's parents knew that he was finding it difficult to settle in and make friends and when they asked him about it, he explained that everyone in his class already had friends and didn't seem interested in making new ones.

George's parents had a word with his teacher, who suggested that he might find it easier to make friends if he joined some after-school clubs. At first George wasn't keen on the idea, but his parents agreed that he wouldn't have to go more than twice if he didn't like it.

The outcome

George started going to an after-school football club and, fortunately, he enjoyed it. He found it easier to make friends outside of the classroom and the club gave him the opportunity to meet more children. He now takes part in a weekly practice and sometimes plays a match at the weekend. He's made a few good friends and now prefers to play outside with them than spend time indoors.

How to improve sports provision at your child's school

Although schools do their best, less than two-thirds of pupils receive the recommended two hours of PE or after-school activities each week. Often this is simply down to a lack of facilities, so if you are concerned about sports provision at your child's school, it's worth talking to the headteacher to find out if there are ways that parents can help. Often, fundraising or volunteer programmes can help to improve the situation – and even something as simple as improving the playground facilities can encourage children to get active during break times.

If your child's headteacher doesn't seem keen to make changes, then don't be put off. Find out if other parents share your concerns and get the Parent-Teacher Association (PTA) involved. Don't be afraid of taking your concerns to the school governors or your Local Education Authority – sometimes you have to go right to the top to make a difference!

10 THINGS TO REMEMBER

1 PE is an important part of your child's curriculum, so it's important to show an interest and encourage your child to work hard.

2 PE can teach your child about teamwork, problem-solving, leadership, concentration and coordination.

3 The government wants all schools to provide at least two hours of physical activity for pupils each week, with the aim to increase this to five hours by 2012.

4 There are 65 per cent of secondary schools and 32 per cent of primary schools that fail to meet these targets, which is why it's important to keep your child active at home.

5 PE lessons for children under the age of seven should focus on fun and teach children how to use and control their growing bodies.

6 From the age of seven, children will gradually be introduced to competitive games.

7 By the age of 11, children will be expected to play sports competitively and compete against their classmates.

8 Joining breakfast and after-school sports clubs can be a great way for children to improve their skills and learn in a more relaxed environment.

9 Practising basic skills at home can help your child to feel more confident in PE classes.

10 Try to give your child the same amount of praise whether they win or lose. Focus on what they did well, and how they can improve next time.

7

Team sports

In this chapter you will learn:
- *how taking part in team sports can benefit your child*
- *which team sports will suit your child*
- *how to find a suitable sports club for your child.*

Most children are introduced to team sports during the second half of their primary education. Although they will have been taught the basic skills involved (throwing, catching and kicking) from the time they start school, children generally don't have the concentration or maturity to understand and follow the rules of a game and play competitively as part of a team until they are seven or eight years old.

The benefits

Around this time, and sometimes even earlier, some children also begin to take part in organized sports outside of school. Many children love playing team games, and need little encouragement to join a local sports club or team. After all, it gives them a great opportunity to spend time with their friends – and make new ones – and it also fosters a great sense of belonging, which is very important to children, as they like to 'fit in' with their peers. Children also respond well to positive attention, so being praised by their coach in front of their teammates, and enjoying the respect and admiration of their peers can help to build their confidence.

Playing team sports can also teach your child many important life lessons, which can benefit them off the playing field. These include learning how to:

▶ *play by the rules*
▶ *respect authority*
▶ *win with grace and lose with dignity*
▶ *take on leadership roles*
▶ *work effectively with others*
▶ *cope with success and failure*
▶ *concentrate and focus.*

For all these reasons, many parents think that team games are the obvious choice when looking for a way to keep their child fit and active – after all, playing as part of a team is also one of the most obvious ways to make exercise fun.

Insight

Joining a sports team can be a great way to help your child make new friends. If your child changes schools or you move to a new area, ask around to find out which clubs are popular with your child's peer group and encourage your child to go along for a taster session.

Sports clubs and coaching sessions can be costly, so before you get started and invest too much time or money, it's a good idea to run through a few practical considerations. Most experts say that children shouldn't specialize in a particular sport too soon, as this can discourage them from trying other activities that they might enjoy more. So give your child lots of opportunities to try different things before they commit to one or two favourites. You should also make sure that your child doesn't have too many demands on their time. It's important that they can keep up with schoolwork, try out any other sports or activities that appeal and have some free time too.

Insight

If your child is under the age of eight, or is new to team sports, it's best to get off to a low-key start. Unless they are really keen to join a club, start out by arranging weekly get-togethers with friends to play football, rounders, cricket – or anything else that takes your fancy. Being part of a team can be too demanding and time-consuming for some children, so wait until they are passionate enough about a sport so that they are happy to commit to the training schedule.

It also pays to be aware that most sports clubs and teams tend to group children according to their age rather than their size, or ability. So if your child is particularly large or small for their age, or is a particularly gifted or nervous participant, check with your local club to make sure that they won't be competing outside their ability. If the competition is too fierce – or too weak – they may lose interest and give up.

Also consider how your child will cope with the demands of organized sports. Regular practice sessions and tournaments are a big commitment, and a talent for kicking a ball doesn't necessarily mean that your child is quite ready to join a football team. Pushing your child to compete before they are ready could put them off team sports for good, so keep the focus on fun until you are certain that your child is ready to take it further.

Finally, it's vital to check that any club you are considering for your child meets the relevant safety standards that are set out at the end of this chapter.

Case study: Helping your child to enjoy team sports

The problem

Willem is a seven-year-old boy who loves football but who is nervous about playing as part of a team. He is in the last year of Infant School, and won't be offered football as part of his PE lessons until he starts Junior School, by which time he will be eight.

(Contd)

He didn't want to wait that long, so he started football practice at a local club. Despite his initial enthusiasm, he didn't seem to take to it very well. His coach told his parents that he was very quiet and reluctant to take part and, as a result, didn't get much opportunity to play in matches.

The solution

Willem's parents, Annabel and Jason, spoke to his coach and discovered that he was the smallest and youngest child on the team. He seemed to lack confidence, was reluctant to play with the other boys and hadn't made any friends on the team. When his parents asked him about it, Willem explained that he was worried that the other boys would think he wasn't any good, and he didn't want to make any mistakes that could cost them a game. As a result, he tended to stay in the background and got bored because he was always expected to play the same position while the other boys got a chance to shine. Willem's parents weren't happy with his coach's approach and attitude, so they asked around and found another club that specialized in teaching younger children.

The outcome

Willem took to the new football club straight away, and gets much more one-to-one attention. As he is no longer the youngest boy on the team, he doesn't feel so self-conscious and now enjoys taking part in weekend matches. He is now much more confident and has formed some strong friendships with other boys in the team.

Which sport is best for my child?

Before you give your child the opportunity to try a new sport, it's wise to think about the following:

- *How much will it cost both to take part and buy the relevant equipment? Is it affordable?*
- *Will my child be able to devote enough time to training and competing?*

- *Does this sport complement my child's personality, body type and sporting abilities? If not, does it matter?*
- *What are the characteristics of the sport? Is there physical contact? Does speed matter more than strength? Does this suit my child?*
- *How will my child get to and from training sessions or tournaments?*

Your answers to these questions should help you to determine which organized sport is most likely to suit your child. But if your child is particularly keen to take part then, if possible, it's best to let them try it and find out for themselves.

Something for everyone?

In light of so many physical, emotional and social benefits, it's tempting to sign your child up for after-school sports clubs, even if they seem reluctant. But it's important to remember that not everyone enjoys team sports. Your child will be required to join in at school, but should never be forced to join extracurricular teams or training sessions in an attempt to improve their skills, as it is more likely to have the opposite effect.

Bear in mind that there is usually a good reason why certain children don't enjoy team games. The most obvious one is that they just don't enjoy a particular sport, so if they really don't want to play football, perhaps they would prefer rugby or hockey instead. Team sports can also seem very complicated to young children who don't understand the rules and even find the line markings on the pitch or court confusing. Joining a beginners club, or even watching an instructional DVD can often be all they need to overcome their initial anxieties.

Sometimes shy children, or those who aren't very confident of their athletic abilities, aren't comfortable being part of a team. Children develop at different rates – both physically and emotionally – so some younger children might not respond well to the discipline and structure of an organized sport. They may also become self-conscious and demoralized when they realize that other children are better at it than they are. This usually causes problems if other children get upset with your child for making a mistake, which may affect the outcome of the game. Explain to your child that it's fine to make mistakes sometimes, and have a word with your child's teacher or coach so that they can keep an eye on the situation.

Not all children are cut out for team sports, but it's worth persuading your child to try out one or two. Make it clear that they don't have to continue with it if they don't want to, but don't use this as an excuse to give up on exercise altogether. Children under the age of ten may just need a little more time to adjust, and grow in confidence before they are ready to play competitively.

If your child is still reluctant to play team sports by the age of 11 or 12, you may have to accept that they will be happier with a different form of exercise. Take a look at the activities outlined in the following chapter.

Is your child cut out for team sports?

Jessica is quite a shy child, and has never been comfortable with team sports. She plays rounders and netball in her PE lessons at school, but doesn't enjoy it at all. She's a perfectly able player but doesn't enjoy the competitive element and prefers activities which she can take part in by herself or with one or two friends. Fortunately, her school offers dance and trampolining – which she loves – so we've encouraged her to focus on those instead. This way she's happy to get fit and active, but she can practise without feeling too much pressure to perform.

Tanya is mum to Jessica, 11.

Good sportsmanship

When children start playing team sports, you need to show your support – which means showing up at the sidelines to watch every match you can. Remember, it really doesn't matter if your child's team wins or loses, so focus on the positives and praise the things your child did right, not the things they did wrong – praise and encourage your child regardless of their performance.

You must think about your own behaviour too. Some parents make terrible spectators and direct critical, negative and hostile remarks at the opposing team, the coach, referee or even their child's teammates and other parents. It's not unusual for parents to swear at the referee, or challenge his decision – and this can be devastatingly embarrassing for your child. Even if you manage to behave yourself on the sidelines, think about how you behave when you are watching televised sport – particularly in front of your child. Even in this context, critical or aggressive comments do not set a good example to young children and do nothing to encourage good sportsmanship. You need to ensure that you are a good role model.

Insight

It's very important that you support your child from the sidelines. If you aren't familiar with the rules of their chosen sport, then ask them to explain it to you and teach you the basic skills involved. They will enjoy being in a position to tell you what to do, and this is a great way to reinforce the skills that they have already learned.

Popular team sports

The best way to encourage an interest in team sports is to practise the basic skills, as outlined in the previous chapter, from an early age. Once children are confident in their abilities they will often ask for the chance to put these skills to work in various sports, or will be introduced to them at school.

However, some schools are only able to offer a limited number of sporting activities – and there may be nothing that particularly appeals to your child. Remember, many schools don't offer certain sports, such as football, until the age of seven or eight, while sports clubs may make them available to children as young as three. Whether or not this is a good idea is open to debate, but if your child shows an interest in a sport, the coaches are fully qualified and the training sessions are age-appropriate, then you could give it a try – but ask for a free trial before you commit, just in case your child doesn't like it.

> **Insight**
> If your child's school doesn't offer a particular sport, then have a word with their PE teacher and find out if it's possible to set up an after-school club. There might even be another parent who has the necessary skills to take on coaching duties.

What follows is a run-down of the most popular team sports for children. Not all of these will be available in schools and some of them have age restrictions, but you should be able to find something to suit your child's personality and abilities. Be sure to play to your child's strengths – fast runners might excel at football, while bigger or slower children might find they have a natural advantage at rugby. Thinking this way can give children a head start – and if they have a good chance of success, they are much more likely to enjoy their sport and want to continue with it.

FOOTBALL

Good for: speed, stamina, coordination and strength.

Many clubs offer lessons and coaching for boys and girls as young as three years old, but Football Association guidelines prevent children under the age of eight from playing in competitive leagues.

The basics: Football is played by two teams of 11 players, although many children's clubs play five-a-side, which not only has fewer players, but is also played on a smaller pitch with smaller goals. This allows children more involvement during the playing time, more individual tuition and more opportunities to score goals. When children start out, they should be given plenty of opportunity to play in different positions, to make sure they get don't get bored.

A normal game of 11-a-side lasts for two halves of 45 minutes. Five-a-side games tend to consist of two halves of 20 minutes.

AMERICAN FOOTBALL

Good for: speed, stamina, coordination and strength.

The basics: American football – or just 'football' as it is known to most Americans – is played by two teams of 11 players, although some schools play with teams of six, eight or nine players.

Although younger players can learn the basic skills involved in the game, American football is primarily played at high school or college, when players are aged 14 and over. The objective is to get to the opponents' 'end zone', which is the area at either end of the field. Teams can score by running the ball into the end zone, or throwing the ball and having it caught in the end zone by a player from the same team. A team can score extra points by kicking the ball between the posts set up in the end zone.

American football is a collision sport, as the defence must tackle the player with the ball by knocking or pulling him down. It has always been associated with a high number of injuries and because of this, players must wear a helmet, shoulder pads, hip pads and kneepads. This amount of protective clothing can leave players vulnerable to heatstroke, so it's vital to make sure that players drink water throughout practice and games.

American football is traditionally a male sport, but women's football is now played on a semi-professional or amateur level in the United States. This has identical rules to its male counterpart and is a full-contact sport, played by all-female teams. As this is a fairly new development, it is offered in very few schools and colleges, but it is occasionally possible for a female player to join the regular male team. However, this doesn't happen often, as differences in size, strength and physical capability can put female players at risk.

The American football season typically lasts for 11 weeks and runs from early September to late November. Most high school games are scheduled for Friday nights. A standard game consists of four 15-minute quarters, but 12-minute quarters are played in high-school football, and quarters can be shorter still for younger players.

RUGBY

Good for: strength, stamina and coordination.

Rugby can be played by boys and girls aged six and over, but most children start out playing either Tag Rugby or Mini Rugby. Some clubs also teach non-contact rugby skills to children as young as two.

The basics: There are two different types of rugby: Rugby League and Rugby Union. League is played by two teams of 13 players, while Union teams have 15 players. Young children often start out playing Tag Rugby, which is a non-contact version of Rugby League, or Mini Rugby, which is a smaller (nine-a-side), simpler version of Rugby Union.

When children start playing rugby, they will have to choose between being a forward or a back. Forwards tend to be larger, stronger and often slower children. Their main role is gaining and retaining possession of the ball, while backs tend to drive the game and typically are more agile, faster and good at kicking the ball.

Rugby League and Rugby Union are both played for two halves of 40 minutes each. Tag Rugby is most usually played for two halves of seven minutes each. However, younger players sometimes play 10-minute games with no half time.

Before your child starts playing, it's important to understand that rugby is a contact sport, so they will have to be prepared to tackle other players and run into the opposition. This means that your child is likely to get a few bumps and bruises during the course of a typical game.

CRICKET

Good for: developing speed of thought, mobility, teamwork and coordination.

Many clubs allow children as young as five to take lessons, but there are other, simpler forms of the game that your child might find more appealing. Kwik Cricket is enjoying a surge of popularity in primary schools, particularly among girls. It is a simple form of the game that uses smaller and lighter equipment, and can be played by children aged five and over. Inter-cricket, which is a soft-ball version of the game, is suitable for children aged 11 and over and is increasingly available in secondary schools and sports clubs. If neither of these are available in your area, then your child might be interested in Urban Cricket. This is a new initiative, designed to appeal to children between seven and twelve years of age. Unlike traditional Cricket, it can be played absolutely anywhere using a plastic bat and tennis ball – you don't even need a pitch.

The basics: Cricket is a bat-and-ball game played by two teams of 11 players. Games are divided into 'overs' of six balls. Each team bats and bowls: the batting team has to score as many runs as possible, while the bowling team tries to stop them and get them 'out'.

Cricket matches can be various lengths. The shortest match is made up of 20 overs a side, known as 20/20, and takes less than three hours to play. One-day games are made up of 50 overs a side and Test Matches are played over five days.

Depending on your child's strength, they may end up being a batsman or a bowler. Batsmen require patience, speed of thought, and coordination, while bowlers need stamina, speed, and imagination.

Cricket is not as fast-paced or explosive as many sports and is often suited to more thoughtful children, although they still need strength and stamina. It also combines individual and teamwork skills, so may appeal to children who don't usually enjoy team sports.

HOCKEY

Good for: coordination, strength and stamina.

There are several forms of hockey, including ice hockey and roller hockey. In the UK and Europe the most common form is field hockey, while ice hockey is more popular in the US and Canada. Hockey can be played by girls and boys, and is often introduced at schools in Year 7, when children are around 11 years old.

England Hockey has recently introduced a brand new game called Quicksticks, which is designed to introduce hockey to primary school children aged seven to eleven. This six-a-side game can be played on any surface and uses a smaller pitch and oversized balls to help beginners learn the basic skills of the game.

The basics: Hockey is an 11-a-side game, which involves manoeuvring a ball into the opponent's net or goal using a hockey stick. The hockey season runs from September to May, and many leagues play weekly matches throughout the season.

A regulation match of field hockey last for 70 minutes, broken into two halves of 35 minutes each. However, most schools play shorter games, and Quicksticks is played for 20–30 minutes, depending on the age of the children playing.

Hockey has a reputation for being a dangerous sport, but most injuries occur as a result of being hit by the ball, so provided your child wears the appropriate safety equipment during practice sessions and matches, the risks should be minimal. Goalkeepers should wear a helmet and pads and all players should wear shin guards and mouthguards. Quicksticks uses a safer, softer ball to make the sport suitable for younger children.

NETBALL

Good for: speed, stamina, coordination, concentration and teamwork.

Netball is a fast-paced, non-contact sport and is a great way to improve general fitness. It is England's biggest female team sport, and is played at most secondary schools. Many clubs run sessions for girls aged seven and over.

The basics: Netball is played on a court with scoring hoops or rings at each end. The objective is to pass the ball to a teammate within the opposition's goal circle, and score a goal. There are seven players on each team (although some junior teams only have five players) who each have named positions, which are displayed on their 'bib'. The only way to move the ball to the goal is to throw it to a teammate – players are not allowed to run with the ball. As players can only move in certain areas of the court, this ensures that everyone is involved in play.

A regulation game of netball lasts for one hour, split into four quarters of 15 minutes. Most schools play shorter games – usually two halves of 15 minutes, so 30 minutes in total.

BASKETBALL

Good for: coordination, control, teamwork and leadership skills.

Basketball is an indoor sport, which is similar to netball. Sometimes referred to as Mini-Basketball, Primary/Under-12 Basketball is played by boys and girls in teams of three, four or five. It can be played from the age of seven, with a view to competing from the age of ten. Once they start secondary school, boys and girls play separately.

The basics: Basketball is a five-a-side game, in which players try to score points against each other by 'shooting' a ball through the opponent's basket. The ball can be moved around the court by bouncing it (dribbling) or passing it between teammates.

The length of the game varies according to the level at which it is played. FIBA (International Basketball Federation) games are played for four 10-minute periods, NBA (National Basketball Association) games are played for four 12-minute periods, and college basketball is played for two 20-minute halves.

Height is an advantage for basketball players, as the hoop is fixed three metres above the ground. Professional players are usually above six foot three inches tall, but shorter players can still be successful players, especially if they can jump to a good height.

ROUNDERS

Good for: coordination, concentration and teamwork.

Rounders is played in most English schools and is one of the most popular summer school sports among both boys and girls. The game has some similarities with Baseball and Softball – it uses similar-sized bats, but has a different pitch layout and does not use baseball-style gloves. Most children are introduced to the sport at primary school and continue to play throughout secondary school. Initially children learn to play with large, flat bats, soft balls or beanbags before progressing to a round bat and tennis balls. Traditional hard rounders balls are seldom used in school sports.

The basics: Rounders is played by two teams, who alternate between batting and fielding. Points, or 'rounders', are scored by the batting team by completing a circuit around the field through four bases or posts, without being put 'out'. The total number of players on a team is limited to 15. A game of rounders lasts for two innings.

Rounders is a fun game that might appeal to children who don't usually enjoy team sports. As players take turns with batting and fielding it helps to have all-round skills. As batters can still run if they don't hit the ball, it's possible for children who are less able at ball games to join in and improve their skills.

BASEBALL

Good for: coordination, concentration and teamwork.

The basics: Baseball is one of the most popular sports in the US and is a popular sport in schools. It is played by two teams of nine players who alternate between batting and catching/pitching the ball. The batting team scores by having a player run across the four 'bases' on the field that form what is called a 'diamond', while the pitching team tries to prevent the batting team from scoring a run.

Many children are introduced to baseball by joining Little League, which organizes local children's leagues of baseball and softball throughout the US. Little League welcomes children between the ages of 5 and 18.

Baseball is one of the few sports not governed by a clock. Instead it lasts for nine 'innings'. In each inning each team member has one turn to bat and score runs before it makes three 'outs'.

....

Are contact sports safe?

Although there is an element of risk involved with almost all forms of sport and activity, the risk of injury is highest in sports that involve contact and collisions. So if your child is keen to play any kind of contact sport, it's very important to take all the recommended precautions to reduce the risk of injury. The following steps should help to reassure you that it's safe for your child to take part:

▶ *Talk to your child's coach and make sure that the focus is on having fun – and steady improvement – rather than competing to win at all costs.*

(Contd)

- ▶ *Make sure that the sports field and all equipment is well maintained and in good condition.*
- ▶ *If your child is small for their age, look for a club that groups children according to ability or size, rather than age. Your child is at greater risk of injury if they are paired with a child who is significantly taller or heavier.*
- ▶ *Ensure your child wears the recommended helmets and safety equipment whenever they are playing, and that it is properly fitted.*
- ▶ *Never push your child to play beyond their ability and listen to any worries or concerns they have about taking part.*
- ▶ *Never allow your child to play with an injury.*

Choosing a club

If your child is serious about getting involved in organized sports, then the best way forward is to join a local sports club or team. The most reliable way to find out about suitable clubs is through word of mouth, so ask other parents for a recommendation, then visit the club yourself so that you can meet the coach and check out the facilities. A well-run club will always be happy to let you look around and ask questions. Alternatively, you could contact the governing body for the sport that your child is interested in, for example the Football Association, as they often publish countrywide lists of recommended clubs.

Before you leave your child in the care of a sports club and its leaders, it's vital to make the following checks:

- ▶ *The coach should have a recognized qualification and should also be trained in child protection and health and safety procedures. They should also have experience dealing with your child's age group.*
- ▶ *All coaches and volunteers should have had a Criminal Records Bureau check. This ensures that they have not*

committed any offence that would make them unsuitable to work with children and young people.

▶ The club should have clear guidelines about physical contact and social relationships between staff, volunteers and participating children. The Criminal Records Bureau check only picks up people who have been caught committing an offence, so it's vital that the club has strict guidelines in place to protect your child.

▶ There should be a written Code of Conduct that sets out what is required of staff and participants and rules out bullying, shouting, racism, sexism or any other unacceptable behaviour.

▶ All equipment should be safe and well maintained.

▶ The facilities should be clean and safe. Find out what precautions are in place to prevent strangers walking in off the street.

▶ If the club is open to boys and girls, male and female staff should be available.

If the club satisfies all the above requirements, the next step is to find out what sort of experience your child will have if they join. It's a good idea to ask the following questions:

▶ What do coaching sessions involve and what does the coach hope to achieve? It's best to look for a club that aims for gradual improvement rather than a succession of wins, as this can create an atmosphere of unhealthy competition.

▶ Will your child get to play in matches even if they are not among the strongest players?

▶ What costs will be involved and will your child need special kit or equipment?

▶ What leagues and tournaments does the team play in and how regularly do they play? This could prove costly or cause transport problems if you have to drive your child to matches.

▶ What is the ratio of staff to children? Young children need more supervision, as do disabled children and children who are playing sports with a higher risk of injury.

Joining a club is the best way to help your child progress in sport and a good coach will know how to get the best out of your child, so provided you take care to make all the necessary checks you should have no grounds for concern. Do make sure that the club has at least two of your contact telephone numbers for use in an emergency, as accidents do happen. And if, at a later date, you have any concerns about the club – for example, you think that your child is being bullied, pushed too hard or seems worried or distressed – be sure to take it up with the coach as soon as possible. Fortunately, serious problems are rare and if your child is happy and looks forward to practices and matches, then you can be confident that all is well.

Insight

When it comes to choosing a club for your child, find out where their friends go. Other parents should be able to give you some tips about the best clubs to try, so visit and have a look around. Ask to meet the coach and then trust your instincts – if you're unsure or uncomfortable then look elsewhere.

Talented athletes

If you child's PE teacher or coach thinks that they have natural talent for a particular sport, you may find that your child is eligible to join a specialist training academy. The Youth Sport Trust is committed to making sure that all talented athletes are given the chance to fulfil their potential. For more information visit http://gifted.youthsporttrust.org/

Getting involved

Make sure you support your child's efforts at all times. If you would like to do more than just cheer from the sidelines, there are many more ways you could get involved. Most clubs rely on some help from volunteers, and there are opportunities to get involved no matter what your sporting ability. Some parents help out with transport and refreshments, but if you are interested in a particular sport you may be able to help out with training sessions – or even train as a coach, manager or referee. There are lots of coaching courses available for different sports and activities, although it does take quite a lot of time and commitment to see it through. Contact the governing body of the sport you are interested in or visit www.sportscoachuk.org for more information. Before you get started, it's a good idea to check how your child would feel about you helping out at their sports club. Some children enjoy the sense of independence they get from spending time away from their family, so make sure that they don't mind you joining in.

TEST YOUR KNOWLEDGE

1 *At what age do most children start playing team games?*

2 *How many players are there in a football team?*

3 *At what age can children start playing football in competitive leagues?*

4 *What are the two different types of rugby?*

5 *At what age can children start playing Kwik Cricket?*

6 *What safety equipment should be worn when your child plays hockey?*

7 *What is the maximum number of players on a rounders team?*

8 *How many innings are there in a game of baseball?*

9 *At what age to children usually learn to play hockey?*

10 *How many players are there in a netball team?*

....

Answers

1 *Seven*

2 *11*

3 *Eight*

4 *Rugby League and Rugby Union*

5 *Five*

6 *Shin guards and mouth guards, and the goalkeeper should wear a helmet and pads*

7 *15*

8 *Nine*

9 *11*

10 *Seven*

8

Individual sports and activities

In this chapter you will learn:
- *why your child might prefer individual sports and activities to team sports*
- *how individual sports and activities can benefit your child*
- *how to identify which individual sports and activities will suit your child.*

Some children are much happier taking part in individual activities than playing team sports. And if you are worried that your child will miss out on some of the benefits of playing as part of a team, then bear in mind that individual sports and activities can also help your child to develop a range of important life skills.

The advantages

Taking part in individual activities can help your child by:

- ▶ *improving confidence and self-belief*
- ▶ *teaching the importance of self-motivation*
- ▶ *increasing patience and building self-discipline through regular practice*
- ▶ *teaching your child how to deal with success and failure*
- ▶ *making them more ambitious*
- ▶ *helping them to set themselves goals and work to achieve them.*

In addition, there are several practical reasons why individual sports and activities might be a better fit for your child than team sports. First and foremost, many children are put off team sports because they don't feel they have the ability to compete against more able children. If they aren't strong players, this means that other children are less likely to want them on their team, and feeling like an unpopular choice can destroy a child's confidence. You may even find yourself in the uncomfortable position of having to explain to your child why they always get stuck playing for the 'bad team' or in the same, perhaps limited, position while other children get the chance to shine. Fortunately, this is never an issue in individual activities, where every child always has the opportunity to showcase their talents and where success is based entirely on their own merit.

Parents should also be aware that some children are reluctant to play team games because they don't understand the rules. Many team games have quite complicated rules and regulations, right down to which specific areas of the pitch or field certain players are allowed to enter. These are sometimes so complex that many adults can't get to grips with them, so it's no wonder that children struggle. For the most part, individual activities tend to have far simpler rules, which makes them much more accessible to younger children. What's more, many can be introduced at a significantly younger age, which can be a definite advantage if you are trying to get you child into the habit of taking regular exercise before they start school.

Insight

Individual activities can be more appealing to children who are shy or uncomfortable in large groups. However, practising alone won't improve your child's social skills or help them to make friends, so it's best to look for a club or group that they can join so that they can spend time with other children too.

Individual activities have another important advantage over team games. Although most team sports, such as football and rugby, are seasonal, many individual activities can be practised all year round. This gives your child more continuity and a much greater opportunity to practise, build their strength and stamina, and add to their expertise.

Unsurprisingly, many parents are delighted to discover that taking part in an individual sport or activity teaches children that regular practice is the key to achieving their goals. However, the frequency and intensity of practice varies from child to child. Some children enjoy taking part in a class once a week but do very little practice at home, while others are keen to practise every day. The amount of time your child devotes to practice sessions is usually influenced by their ability and personal goals – if your child is very serious about their sport, they will need to put in the hours in order to compete at a high level. However, most children are only interested in having fun, so it's not necessary to encourage them to practise more than once or twice a week unless they really want to.

If your child is determined to practise every day, you may want to encourage them to slow down. Too much practice can be a bad thing as it not only increases your child's risk of injury and potentially puts their growing body under too much strain, but it also leaves little time for your child to do anything else. Training too hard can harm your child physically, emotionally and socially, so make sure that they have lots of time to rest, relax and have fun with friends.

Practice makes perfect

Niall started judo when he was eight. At first I was reluctant to let him join a class as I thought that martial arts were dangerous, but I did some research, had a chat to the instructor and decided to let him try it out. Niall isn't a particularly sporty child, but he enjoys judo and always comes home and shows us what he's learned. He was awarded his first 'belt' – a yellow belt – after a few months and he was so proud of himself. He's now working towards his orange belt, and hopes to get it by the end of the year. Judo has taught him that he can reach his goals if he tries hard enough, and he's much more confident in his abilities as a result.

Sylvia is mum to Niall, ten.

Going it alone

Before you introduce your child to individual sports or activities, it's a good idea to consider one or two potential drawbacks. First, individual sports don't offer your child as much opportunity to interact and bond with other children. Although your child may well make new friends if they join a gymnastics club or take dance classes, the emphasis will be on acquiring skills and building individual talents rather than team building. As a result, your child is less likely to build strong friendships in this context, and will probably practise by themselves, rather than with other children. Less outgoing children may well prefer this, but if you are keen to boost your child's social skills and help them to feel more comfortable in a group situation, then participating in individual sports and activities is unlikely to help – and may even hinder your child's social development.

Your child may also find it harder to deal with failure without the support of a team. If your child's team performs badly, then players usually accept joint responsibility, but if your child is competing on an individual basis, they may find it difficult to cope with their disappointment if they don't achieve their goals, particularly if they have worked very hard and tried their best. It can be tough for a child to accept that others are more skilled than they are, but you can help prevent this becoming a problem by focusing on steady improvement rather than winning. If there is too much emphasis on coming first, your child may crumble under the pressure, so try to get them in the habit of competing against themselves – by improving time, performance and skills – rather than competing against other children.

You may also find that individual sports offer fewer opportunities for structured practice sessions. Usually, your child will be expected to practise in their own time, which inevitably means that some children won't put in the necessary effort to improve their performance, or even to keep fit. If this happens with your child, then you may want to investigate why they are reluctant to practise. Perhaps they find the sport or activity boring, or are disillusioned by their lack of ability. If this is the case, it may be time to look for another sport or activity that they will enjoy more.

Finding an activity to suit your child

If you're trying to come up with an activity that your child might enjoy, the following questions might help:

▶ *What are your child's hobbies and interests? Have they shown an interest in any sports or activities, even as a spectator?*
▶ *What is your child good at? Are they a fast runner, good at hitting a ball or naturally graceful?*
▶ *Would your child like to compete?*
▶ *Can you afford private lessons or specialist equipment?*
▶ *How much time does your child have to practise?*

Jot down your answers, and then read through the list of suggested activities on the following pages to see which of them best fit your child's requirements.

Case study: Dealing with a child who gets bored quickly

The problem

Shannon is an 11-year-old girl who gives up every activity she tries within weeks. She has tried several sports and activities but usually loses interest quickly. Her parents, Sharon and Antony, are keen for her to exercise, so encourage her as much as they can, but they are starting to get fed up with wasting time and money on lessons and sporting equipment, only for Shannon to get bored. In the last year alone they have tried dance classes, rollerblading and horse riding and are starting to run out of ideas.

The solution

Most parents will go through this with their child at some point. Frustrating as it is, at least it shows parents that their child is

(Contd)

interested in being active, even if they haven't yet found an activity they enjoy.

Rather than spending lots of money on another costly activity, Shannon's parents asked her to think about what she enjoyed doing in school sports. Although she didn't like team sports, she loved swimming and was a fast runner. So Shannon's parents decided that the best way forward was to build on her existing skills rather than start something new.

The outcome

Shannon joined the local athletics club and also began weekly swimming sessions to help her improve her performance. As she already had some ability, Shannon was able to progress very quickly, and this kept her interested. Thanks to regular training, she can run faster, and she's also doing her Amateur Swimming Association (ASA) Awards, so she's always got a new goal to keep her motivated.

Weighing up the options

Different sports require different skills, but there are so many options that you should be able to find something that your child can enjoy. Many individual activities can be played competitively or just for fun – so if your child doesn't cope well with pressure, make sure that they won't be expected to compete.

If your child still insists that they 'don't like sport', then try to come up with a list of activities that you think they might enjoy and ask them to choose something they would be willing to try. Think about your child's natural abilities, how they like to spend their time and whether they are outgoing or shy. Be sure to include a few 'non sporting' activities such as dance or even active computer games, and you may find it easier than you expected to win them over.

Insight

Individual activities are particularly well-suited to children who are overweight, unfit or lacking in confidence. Help your child to identify an activity they could try – it could be something as simple as walking or swimming – and then monitor their progress on a weekly basis. They will benefit from the confidence boost that comes from learning new skills or improving their performance.

When looking for a sport that your child will enjoy, don't assume that you have to choose between team sports and individual activities: your child can do both. Some children like playing as part of a team and taking part in individual sports, and you should do everything you can to encourage this. You may also find that a child who initially expresses reservations about joining a team changes their mind after practising an individual sport. Often this is simply because their fitness and self-confidence has improved, but it can also be because they are able to transfer some of the skills they have learned. For example, a child who enjoys racquet sports such as tennis or badminton may find that they become more confident about hitting the ball in rounders. Just take care that your child doesn't take on too much, or the pressure of regular practice sessions and matches may become tiring for the whole family.

Getting kitted out

Many children will need to try out a variety of sports and activities before they find the perfect fit – and there's every chance that they will greet every new activity with enthusiasm only to lose interest within weeks. If your child has a tendency to do this, try not to get irritated or force them to stick with an activity they don't enjoy, but equally don't be talked into paying for expensive equipment or committing to a block booking of lessons until you are sure your child is going to stick with it. Instead, find out if you can hire any necessary equipment or borrow it from friends – and look for clubs that offer a free trial before you commit. This should give you enough time to decide if your child is going to enjoy it before you spend too much money.

Insight

When your child starts a new activity, it's best to borrow or buy second-hand equipment to start with. You could then set specific targets and agree to buy the new equipment when your child meets them. This gives your child the opportunity to prove their commitment – and a tangible goal to aim for.

Try to remember that when your child starts a new sport or activity, they will almost certainly pester you to buy them new clothes and equipment so that they look the part. Although this may seem like a waste of money to you, be sensitive to their feelings. Appearances matter to children, especially as they approach their teens, and being forced to wear unfashionable clothes or use battered, old equipment can make them feel embarrassed and self-conscious – and could even be enough to put them off altogether. There's no need to spend a fortune on designer sportswear or top-of-the-range equipment, but allowing your child to choose their own gear can help to boost their enthusiasm and make them feel happier and more confident about taking part.

Popular individual sports

The following activities detailed should help you to work out what might appeal to your child. You might find that not all these activities are available at your child's school, but classes or organized sessions should be on offer at sports clubs or leisure centres. Of course, you can introduce your child to some of these activities – such as cycling or swimming – without any lessons or structured sessions. However, if you decide to teach your child yourself, make sure that you have the necessary patience, the right equipment, know what you are doing and don't pass on any bad – or potentially dangerous – habits. If you have any doubts about your own ability, organize one or two introductory lessons, just to teach your child the basics.

SWIMMING

Good for: cardiovascular fitness, strength and stamina.

Swimming is an important – not to mention potentially life-saving – skill for children to master. Unlike some other sports, it's never too early or too late to start and it's the perfect form of exercise for children who are unable to take part in other sports due to health problems or disabilities.

The basics: This is one sport where you can really help your child, so try to get into the habit of making regular trips to your local pool before your child starts school. At first, focus on having fun and splashing around in the water – the sooner you can get them used to the water, the more confident they are likely to be. You may also like to think about organized swimming lessons. Most swimming pools have a range of classes suitable for small babies, toddlers and children. For more on this, turn to Chapter 3.

According to government standards, children should be able to swim 25 metres, use a variety of different swimming strokes and have completed a series of exercises in swimming and floating by the time they are 11 years old. Most schools follow a programme of swimming awards, such as the Amateur Swimming Association (ASA) Awards. This awards scheme covers everything from building confidence in the water as a non-swimmer in Stage 1, right up to swimming distances of up to 150 metres and using competitive swimming strokes in Stage 12.

If your child is a strong swimmer, then they might enjoy taking part in competitions. Some schools have a swim team. If your child's doesn't, then you may have to join a local club or leisure centre.

Did you know?
Research from the *Times* Educational Supplement has revealed that over one-third of children can't swim by the time they leave primary school.

ATHLETICS

Good for: speed, stamina and coordination.

Athletics is a three-part sport combining running, jumping or throwing. Most children are introduced to athletics at school, usually when they are around the age of eight. By this age most children already have a good grasp of the basic skills involved and, as they can practise anywhere with minimal equipment, it's a great, low-cost way to get active – and get some fresh air at the same time.

The basics: Athletics is primarily a summertime sport. It is made up of various running events (sprints, middle and long distance, cross-county, hurdles), jumping (high jump, long jump and triple jump) and throwing (javelin, discus and shot-put). When children are at primary school, the focus should be firmly on fun and they should only run short distances, up to a maximum of 400 metres. Older children will be encouraged to compete, sometimes as part of a team. In this respect, children who take part in athletics get the best of both worlds – the opportunity to compete as an individual, and also become part of an athletics team.

TENNIS

Good for: hand–eye coordination, speed, stamina and concentration.

Tennis is traditionally a summer sport, although it can be played all year round on indoor courts. Mini Tennis is aimed at children aged four to ten, and is played on a smaller court with low nets, using soft balls and usually plastic racquets.

The basics: Tennis can be played either between two opposing players (singles), two teams of two opposing players each (doubles), or two teams of two with a male and female player in each (mixed doubles). Players use a racquet to hit the ball over the net and into the other player's court. Each point starts with a serve, and when the ball is hit, a rally begins. The first player who can't

return the ball loses that point. The first player to win four points –
and at least two more than their opponent – wins the game, and
the first player to win six games – and at least two more than their
opponent – wins the set. The player who wins the best of three sets
(or sometimes five sets in major events) is the winner.

If your child would like to learn how to play tennis, you shouldn't
find it difficult to find a club that gives lessons in your area. To
give them a taster, you could always take them to your local tennis
courts and show them how to hit a ball – or even play swingball in
your garden.

BADMINTON

Good for: stamina, speed, agility and hand–eye coordination.

Badminton is an indoor racquet sport played by two opposing
players (singles), two opposing pairs (doubles) or two pairs with
a male and female player in each (mixed doubles). It's a good
introduction to racquet sports as the shuttlecock is designed to
slow down and float in the air, making it easier to hit than a ball.
Badminton racquets are substantially lighter than tennis racquets,
which means that the sport requires less upper body strength. For
these reasons, children as young as three years old can be taught
the basics, but it is seldom offered in schools until Year 6 or 7.

The basics: Badminton is played using a shuttlecock – a cone-
shaped object with a rounded tip. Unlike tennis, the shuttlecock
is not allowed to bounce and serving players can only hit it
underhand (upwards) without raising the racquet above waist
level. Players score a point every time they win a rally on their own
serve, and each game is played up to 21 points. If the players tie,
the game continues until one player achieves a two-point lead, up
to a maximum of 30 points. The player who wins the best of three
games wins the match. Although badminton can be played at a
very high level, it's a great sport for children who are not confident
about their ability as even complete beginners can get the hang of

it within minutes. If your child shows a particular talent for the sport, they can begin to compete from the age of 11.

GYMNASTICS

Good for: flexibility, balance, coordination and concentration.

Gymnastics is a popular sport with children. Toddlers can learn the basics as soon as they can walk, thanks to activity classes such as Tumbletots or Gymboree. Children are usually introduced to basic gymnastics as soon as they start school, and steadily progress to more complex moves, both on the floor and using apparatus. If your child shows a particular interest or ability, they could join a gymnastics club, where they can train for proficiency awards.

The basics: Gymnastics encompasses a range of activities, which vary for boys and girls. Accomplished male gymnasts tend to perform on the horizontal bar, parallel bars, pommel horse and rings. They also do floor exercises and vault. Female gymnasts do the floor exercises and vault, as well as the balance beam and uneven bars. Gymnastics also incorporates trampolining and cheerleading – both tend to be particularly popular with girls who are reluctant to take part in other sports.

When taking part in gymnastics, children should be taught to warm up and stretch to prevent injury. Soft mats should always be used underneath apparatus to protect your child in the event of a fall.

DANCING

Good for: overall fitness, balance, posture and coordination.

Dance and movement is taught in schools, but some dance schools offer basic introductory lessons to children as young as two. Most parents assume that dancing is for girls, but this is not at all the case. The increasing popularity of street dance and hip hop have made it much more appealing for boys – and thanks to the success of films such as *Billy Elliot* it's no longer so unusual for boys to take lessons in ballet.

The basics: Children can choose from a range of different types of dance, many of which can be taught to children aged four and over. Before choosing a class for your child, think about their personality and the type of music they enjoy. This should help you to pinpoint the most suitable type of dance.

▶ *Ballet: This is usually set to classical music and involves precise movements and perfect posture. Classes are quite disciplined, which can be very good for some children, but may not suit others. Ballet increases strength, balance and flexibility and is a good foundation for other types of dance.*
▶ *Tap: This is an energetic style of dance, which requires your child to tap their feet in time to the music. Special shoes with metal 'taps' will be required and your child will be taught sequences of steps and moves, which will build coordination and rhythm.*
▶ *Ballroom: More children are becoming interested in ballroom dancing as a result of the popular television shows such as* Strictly Come Dancing *and* Dancing With The Stars. *Children start by learning classic dances such as the waltz, foxtrot, rumba and tango. Ballroom dancing can be fiercely competitive and if your child wishes to compete, costumes can be expensive.*
▶ *Jazz: This is usually popular with children as it is much more relaxed than ballet and is set to upbeat, energetic music. This is a particularly creative form of dance, so there is lots of flexibility in terms of the moves that your child will perform.*
▶ *Hip Hop: Hip Hop classes are popular with older children because they give them the opportunity to dance to hip hop, funk and rap – which is often the type of music that they enjoy listening to with friends. The style of dance is modern and creative, so it's a great choice for children with lots of energy and imagination.*
▶ *Irish: This traditional form of dance involves keeping a stiff and straight upper body while performing complex steps. Dances are performed to Irish music such as jigs and reels.*
▶ *Modern: This is a technical form of modern dance that is great for coordination and balance. It's not recommended for beginners, but will help children with some experience of dance to create their own style.*

Before your child starts classes, it's also a good idea to think about whether they would like to take examinations or compete. Most dance schools encourage children to take the Royal Academy of Dance (RAD) examinations, but these are not compulsory. Most children enjoy practising for – and passing – their exams, but don't push your child into doing so if they are particularly nervous or worried about it.

Most classes also put on regular shows, so it's wise to think about how your child will feel about performing in front of an audience. If your child is very shy and self-conscious, this may put them off – but it could also help them to develop some much needed self-confidence.

Insight

Most young children enjoy dancing, and it's a great form of exercise. But dance lessons can be expensive, and you can improve your child's fitness just by dancing at home. Get into the habit of turning on the radio and moving to the music when you're in the kitchen doing the dishes or getting dressed in the morning. Even dancing for ten minutes will help to keep you and your family active.

MARTIAL ARTS

Good for: strength, flexibility, coordination, confidence, self-esteem and self-control.

Martial arts have become increasingly popular with children, largely because they feature so frequently in television, film and computer games. Many parents worry that these sports are too violent for children, but when properly taught they are very safe. Most clubs will offer classes for boys and girls aged eight and over, but some will teach the basics to children as young as six.

The basics: There are several martial arts that are popular with children. The following list should help you to identify the one most suited to your child.

- ▶ *Judo: This is considered to be the safest of the martial arts, and focuses a great deal on mental and moral development. It features moves similar to wrestling and is a popular introduction to the martial arts for children.*
- ▶ *Karate: This is intended as a form of self-defence, which incorporates throws, punches, kicks and blocking.*
- ▶ *Kung Fu: This is based around a series of kicks, chops and punches, which are aimed at particular pressure points on an opponent's body.*
- ▶ *Ju-jitsu: This is one of the oldest of the martial arts, and involves sparring and the use of some weapons.*
- ▶ *Tae kwon do: This incorporates striking and high kicks to score points against an opponent.*
- ▶ *Aikido: This is a non-competitive and rather more spiritual option. The focus is on fending off attacks and turning the tables on the aggressor.*

Children who are small, shy or lacking in confidence may benefit most from learning a martial art, as it is a great way to build confidence and physical strength. This is particularly helpful for children who have been victims of bullying as it may help them to overcome their nervousness and feel less vulnerable.

FENCING

Good for: strength, balance and agility.

Fencing is a game of swordplay. Opponents use one of three light, flexible weapons: a 'foil', a 'sabre' or an 'epée'. The foil is the most commonly used and the one children tend to start with. Fencing is an increasingly popular sport, and many schools, sports clubs and leisure centres offer classes to children aged six and over. Children's fencing classes are usually based around a range of games to improve speed and coordination, teach basic blade and footwork and develop tactical thinking. Boys and girls train together and are encouraged to compete as their skills develop.

The basics: Fencers wear masks and protective clothing and move forward and back, using different techniques to try to score points, hitting their opponent on the body with the end of the weapon. It is performed in 'bouts', which are performed on a long, thin strip called a 'piste'. Each bout must stop after three minutes of fencing, or when one fencer has reached the required number of points needed to win.

Fencing is ideal for children who don't enjoy traditional school sports, and is particularly popular with thoughtful children who enjoy developing the tactical and intellectual skills needed to outwit their opponent. Provided a qualified teacher is supervising, and the correct clothing and safety equipment is worn, fencing is a very safe sport and the risk of even minor injury is minimal.

ARCHERY

Good for: upper body strength, focus, coordination, patience and self-confidence.

Archery is a sport where a bow is used to shoot an arrow at a target from a set distance. Points are awarded according to the accuracy of each shot. Some schools offer lessons in archery, and clubs offer lessons to children over the age of nine. Before this age, most children are unable to handle the equipment properly.

The basics: The most popular form of archery is Target Archery, where arrows are shot at a target for accuracy. Target Archery competitions may be held indoors or outdoors. Targets are marked with ten evenly spaced concentric rings, which have score values from one to ten assigned to them, along with an inner ten ring, sometimes called the 'X ring'. Competition is divided into 'ends' of three or six arrows. Archers have a set time limit in which to shoot all their arrows, before walking to the target and working out their score. The archer with the highest score wins.

Equipment is usually available for hire, so it shouldn't be too expensive to get started. It's important to be aware that archery can be a dangerous sport if participants are reckless, so children should be mature enough to understand the need to behave responsibly at all times.

ICE-SKATING

Good for: strength, posture, flexibility and balance.

Ice-skating can be enjoyed for fun or as a competitive sport, and is becoming increasingly popular thanks to the success of television shows such as *Dancing On Ice*. If your child is serious about skating, many rinks offer lessons to children over the age of five.

The basics: There are several forms of competitive ice-skating. These are:

▶ *Singles figure skating: This is where men or women perform a routine that is judged on technical merit and showmanship.*
▶ *Pairs skating: This is performed in mixed pairs. Skaters perform choreographed programmes which include overhead lifts and throws.*
▶ *Ice dancing: Again, this is performed in mixed pairs. It does not feature the complicated jumps and lifts that are part of figure skating, and has a greater emphasis on how skaters move to the music.*
▶ *Synchronized skating: This involves teams of skaters performing a synchronized routine.*
▶ *Speed skating: This involves sprinting on ice for a set distance. The fastest skater wins.*

The best way to get started is to find a rink that offers the National Ice Skating Association (NISA) Ten Step Learn to Skate programme. This covers basic skating instruction to get your child upright on the ice, and helps to identify talented young skaters who may have the ability to take it further.

....
Insight
Many large towns and cities now open outdoor ice rinks during the winter months, and this can be a great way to

(Contd)

introduce children to the sport. Make an occasion of it and
go skating as a family – if your child enjoys it, look for a
local indoor rink where they can practise all year round.

COMPUTER GAMES

If you struggle to stop your child playing computer games from
morning until night, then don't despair – you can still get them
active. The Nintendo Wii games console actually requires players
to get up and move about, as the movements of the handheld
remote are reflected on the screen. This means that players can
participate in virtual games of tennis, golf, football and a range of
other sports without leaving the house. Players can also buy the
Wii Balance Board, which can monitor performance, and provide
tips to improve technique, as players practise strength training,
aerobics, yoga and balance games.

10 THINGS TO REMEMBER

1 *Individual activities can help your child to develop self-discipline and self-motivation.*

2 *Individual activities tend to have simpler rules, which makes them more accessible for younger children.*

3 *Most individual activities can be practised all year round, which gives your child much more opportunity to develop their skills.*

4 *Don't push your child to practise if they don't want to, but encourage them to work on their skills at least once per week.*

5 *Your child is less likely to build strong friendships if they are not part of a team, so encourage them to join a group or club so that they get plenty of opportunity to mix with other children.*

6 *Focus on steady improvement rather than winning, otherwise your child may feel that they are under too much pressure to have fun.*

7 *Sports and activities can be time-consuming, so make sure that your child has enough free time to relax and play with friends.*

8 *If your child loves computer games, then think about introducing them to the Wii Fit, so that they can exercise as they play.*

9 *Encourage your child to compete against themselves rather than against other children.*

10 *Make sure that your child doesn't train too hard. Practising too much can put their growing body under a great deal of strain.*

9

Problems and concerns

In this chapter you will learn:
- *how to make exercise safe for growing children*
- *how to identify the most common sporting injuries*
- *how to help children with health problems to get fit*
- *how to find sports and activities to suit children with disabilities.*

All parents worry about their children, and this chapter is designed to address the most common problems and concerns that you may face when helping your child to get fit. In this chapter you will find information about how exercise can affect your child's growing body. Although regular exercise can benefit your child in lots of different ways, it's a good idea to read through this section and discover the best ways to avoid injury or prevent your child from overdoing it.

Before your child begins any new sport or activity, make sure that it's safe for them to participate. Some sports and activities carry more risks than others, although these can usually be significantly reduced with proper instruction and supervision and the use of the recommended safety equipment. But, as all parents know, accidents do happen, so you will also find out how to identify the most common injuries, along with advice on how to treat them. There's also information on the ways in which sport and activities can benefit children with illnesses such as asthma and diabetes.

All parents worry about their children, but try not to let your fears and anxieties limit your child's experiences. Accidents do happen, but if your child is receiving proper instruction and is using the correct safety equipment, the risks should be minimal. Resist the urge to wrap your child in cotton wool, as the benefits of taking part in sports and activities significantly outweigh the risks.

Along with minimizing the risk of accident and injury, you need to consider your child's emotional wellbeing. Participating in sports should be fun, but some children can be put off by a negative experience. Sadly, bullying is not uncommon in sports, and although most schools and clubs have implemented strict guidelines on how to deal with the problem, they can only help if you or your child asks them to. Many children are too embarrassed to admit that they are victims of bullying, so it's important to know how to spot the signs that suggest your child is being targeted.

At the end of this chapter, you will find information specifically for parents whose children are disabled. Many sports and activities can be adapted to make them accessible to disabled children, and you will find information on the best way to get your child involved.

Safe exercise for growing children

Before you introduce your child to regular exercise, try to understand that children's and adult's bodies react to physical activity in different ways. Children can't perform at the same level as adults for several reasons:

▶ *Children lack coordination and have slower reaction times than adults. This is simply because their bodies are still growing and developing, but it does make them more accident-prone.*

- *Children have less stamina than adults. This is because they have lower reserves of power and their bodies cannot sustain the energy needed to be active for an extended period of time. This is why children get tired very quickly and can only manage short bursts of intense exercise before stopping for a rest.*
- *Children's muscles are not as strong as adults, which is why they can't run as fast or jump as high. For this reason, activities aimed at increasing strength and building muscle – such as weight training – are not suitable until puberty has ended.*
- *Children do not cope well with extremes of temperature, because their internal temperature control mechanisms are not fully developed. This means that they are more likely to overheat, particularly in hot weather. It's best to limit the amount of exercise young children take during the hottest part of the day. They should sip cool drinks every 20–30 minutes throughout play to prevent dehydration and should always take extra time to cool down afterwards. Children are also at risk in cold weather, so make sure that they are adequately dressed when spending time outdoors in winter.*
- *Children's bodies are still growing, so they are more susceptible to injury. Their muscles, tendons and ligaments are not as strong and they have weaker bones, which break more easily. Although most injuries occur as a result of an accident or fall, over-training can also cause problems, so it's important to make sure your child isn't pushed too hard.*
- *Young children are not very good at assessing risk. This means that they are more likely to put themselves in danger or attempt to do things that are beyond their capabilities.*

For the reasons set out above, don't expect children to perform in the same way as adults, as this could increase the risk of injury. There are several more practical steps you can take to minimize the risks:

- *If your child is new to a particular sport or activity, make sure that they know what they're doing – and what they shouldn't do. Parents, teachers or coaches should explain the rules of* the game so that children are not caught off guard or put themselves or other children at risk.

▶ Children should wear the necessary protective clothing, which should be properly fitted and well maintained.

▶ Children should be taught to warm up and cool down, before and after playing sports.

▶ Injuries associated with overuse are common among children who focus exclusively on one sport. Encourage your child to participate in a range of activities to reduce the risk.

▶ Children should always be supervised when playing sports. This ensures that they are not putting themselves or other children at risk and do not continue to play if they have been injured.

▶ Children should never continue to play if they are in pain. Even minor injuries should be checked and given the necessary time to heal before your child resumes their sporting activities.

▶ Equipment and pitches or areas of play should be scaled down wherever possible to make them suitable for younger children.

▶ Proper coaching can teach children how to fall properly to reduce the risk of injury.

▶ Children should wear a high SPF sunscreen whenever they play sports outside in summer.

▶ Parents and coaches shouldn't push children to take part in sports and activities if they are tired or unwell.

▶ Playing fields should be well maintained so that they are not uneven or full of holes or ruts that may cause children to trip or fall. Where possible, avoid playing on concrete surfaces, as this can increase the risk of injury if your child does take a tumble.

▶ Don't allow your child to take part in sports or activities if they are unwell.

Insight

Pay attention to your child's physical and emotional wellbeing, and don't push them to work harder than they comfortably can. Children who excel at sports often feel tremendous pressure to succeed, so encourage them to take a break or cut back on training if they seem overtired or unhappy.

Warming up and cooling down

It's important to teach your child to warm up before doing any kind of sport or exercise. Gentle warm-up exercise increases the heart rate and increases blood flow around the body. This takes oxygen to the muscles, tendons and ligaments, which makes it easier to stretch and move around without discomfort, stiffness or injury. Follow the steps below for a simple but effective warm-up.

1 *Jog on the spot for a few minutes to warm up the body and increase the heart rate.*
2 *Swing the arms and legs in big circles to loosen up the joints.*
3 *Gently stretch to improve flexibility and warm up the different muscles in the arms and legs. Your child's PE teacher or coach will be able to show them how to do this correctly.*
4 *Your child is now warmed up and ready to play.*

When your child has finished exercising, they should spend a few minutes cooling down. This allows the heart rate to gradually return to normal and helps to stretch tired muscles and prevent soreness and stiffness. Follow the steps below to help your child cool down.

1 *Gradually reduce the speed and intensity of activity. For example, reduce a run to a jog and then to a walk.*
2 *Repeat the warm-up stretches, but hold them for 15–20 seconds.*
3 *When breathing and heart rate has returned to normal, the body feels cooler and perspiration is beginning to dry, the cool down is complete.*

Common injuries and treatment

The injuries that children sustain while taking part in sports and physical activities fall into two broad types:

▶ *acute injuries*
▶ *overuse injuries.*

Acute injuries, such as cuts, bruises, sprains, strains and broken bones, are usually caused by sudden trauma, such as a fall. Overuse injuries are caused by repetitive use of one, or one group of muscles. Typical injuries include muscle tears, minor fractures or progressive bone problems.

The medical advice offered in this book is a guideline only, and is not intended as a substitute for proper medical advice or supervision. So if your child is injured when playing sport, or complains of sustained pain, stiffness or discomfort, then it's always advisable to get them checked over by a doctor. If the injury affects your child's ability to move a particular part of their body – for example, if they can't bend their finger or walk without limping – then you should take them to your local hospital for an examination and X-ray.

Head injuries, particularly those that cause your child to lose consciousness, should always be taken very seriously, so take your child to your local emergency department to make sure that they haven't suffered a concussion. If your child suffers a sharp blow to the chest or torso, they should also be checked over by a doctor.

What follows is a brief guide to some of the most common sporting injuries, along with information on how to spot them and how they should be treated.

Insight

Most parents wouldn't know how to cope with a medical emergency, so look into taking a beginners or refresher course in first aid. Most courses cover everything from dealing with cuts and grazes, to CPR and learning these skills will help you to stay calm and focused when your child sustains the inevitable bumps and bruises.

CUTS AND GRAZES

Most parents get used to treating cuts and bruises when their children are small and unsteady on their feet. In most cases treatment is straightforward, but serious cuts will need medical attention.

Treatment
Bleeding from small cuts and grazes can be stopped by applying pressure using a sterile dressing or clean cloth, and elevating the affected area. The area should then be cleaned with an antiseptic solution and dressed or bandaged.

You must seek medical attention if: there is a lot of blood or bleeding does not stop within ten minutes; there is something embedded in the cut; the skin was punctured; or the wound is deep. This is because the wound may need to be cleaned and stitched to prevent infection and aid healing. You also need to check with your doctor if the cut doesn't seem to be healing or appears to be infected.

SPRAINS

A sprain is a stretch or tear of a ligament. Ligaments are the strong bands of tissue around joints that connect one bone to another and help to keep them stable. If your child suffers a sprain, one or more of these ligaments have been stretched, twisted or torn. The most common locations for a sprain are the ankle, thumb and wrist.

How to spot them: A sprained ankle is a fairly common injury, usually caused by twisting or turning the ankle inwards. This leads to swelling, bruising and pain around the joint. The swelling will occur very quickly, but it may take some time for a bruise to develop. If you suspect that your child has suffered a sprain, it's best to see a doctor to rule out any other injuries and ensure that it is healing properly.

Treatment
Immediate treatment of a sprain should use RICE therapy. This involves:

- ► *Rest: It's important to stop the activity that caused the injury and rest the affected area. Two days of rest is recommended.*
- ► *Ice: Apply an ice pack to the area for 10–30 minutes. A bag of frozen peas wrapped in a tea towel will work just as well, but*

*make sure the ice doesn't touch the skin directly, as this may
cause a burn. Don't apply if the skin is broken.*

▶ *Compression: Applying a bandage (or tubigrip) to the area
will help to limit swelling.*

▶ *Elevation: The affected area should be elevated to a
comfortable height, particularly at night. This helps to reduce
swelling by draining away excess fluid.*

Symptoms should improve after a few days, but some sprains can
take weeks to heel completely.

STRAINS

A strain is a twist, pull or tear of a muscle or tendon – the tough
tissue at the end of a bone that connects it to muscle. Strains are
caused by over-stretching or over-contracting a muscle, and are
fairly common injuries, particularly in sports that involve running,
jumping or changes of direction. Strains can result from overuse as
well as a sudden or acute injury.

How to spot them: The main symptoms are swelling and pain, but
strains can also cause muscle spasm and a loss of strength in the
muscle. Common examples of strains are tendon strains around the
ankle and low back strain. A hamstring strain can also occur when
the hamstring muscle at the back of the thigh is stretched beyond
its limit.

Treatment
First-aid treatment should follow the RICE method (see earlier),
but your child should also see a doctor to rule out any other
injuries. Your doctor may recommend resting the area for several
weeks, and in some cases may refer your child to a physiotherapist.

TORN CARTILAGE

Cartilage is a tough, flexible tissue that covers the surface of
joints and acts as a shock absorber. It allows bones to slide over
each other without creating friction and also helps to support

your weight when you move, run, bend or stretch. Cartilage damage can occur as a result of a sudden, direct blow such as a bad fall directly onto the knees, or a bad tackle in football or rugby.

How to spot it: The symptoms of a torn cartilage include swelling, pain, stiffness and an inability to move the joint. It's also common for the knee to lock or to give way when bearing weight. You must get this kind of injury checked out by a doctor as it can be potentially serious if not properly diagnosed and treated.

Treatment
Unlike other forms of tissue, cartilage does not have a blood supply, so it does not heal as quickly as damaged skin or muscles. Small tears to the cartilage can usually be cured by rest and/or physiotherapy. More serious tears may require surgery.

BROKEN BONES

A broken or cracked bone is known as a fracture. Bones can fracture in a number of different ways, but as children's bones are softer than adults' they don't usually break all the way through. Instead they tend to fracture on one side but bend on the other. This is known as a greenstick fracture.

How to spot them: The symptoms of a fracture depend on the severity of the injury. There will usually be pain and swelling, the affected limb or body part may be bent at an unusual angle, and it's likely that the sufferer won't be able to move or put any weight on the injured area. A person who has broken a bone may seem pale and clammy and may feel faint, dizzy or sick. Fractures can usually be diagnosed through examination alone, but the diagnosis will be confirmed by an X-ray.

Treatment
Greenstick fractures almost always heal well. The doctor will realign the broken bone and apply a cast to hold the bones in the correct position while they heal. A cast usually has to be worn for anything from three to eight weeks, depending on the bone involved.

More serious fractures may sometimes require surgery to repair the damage, but this is very rare.

GROWTH PLATE INJURIES

As children's bones are still growing, they are at risk of potentially serious growth plate injuries. Growth plates are the areas of developing cartilage where bone growth occurs in children and young people. When growth is complete – sometime in adolescence – these growth plates turn into solid bone. Until then, the growth plate is the weakest part of the developing skeleton – even weaker than the nearby tendons and ligaments. For this reason, an accident that would usually cause a sprain in adults could result in a growth plate injury in a child.

How to spot them: Most injuries to the growth plate are fractures. They occur twice as often in boys as in girls, and almost half of them occur in the lower end of the forearm, at the wrist. These injuries also occur frequently in lower bones of the leg, ankle, foot, upper leg or hip bone. Most growth plate injuries occur as a result of a fall or blow to a limb. But they can also result from overuse – so children who train for hours are particularly at risk.

If your child has an accident during play, or experiences persistent pain or discomfort, which affects their ability to move or put pressure on a limb, then it's a good idea to get them checked over by a doctor.

Treatment

Growth plate injuries are usually diagnosed through examination and an X-ray or an MRI scan. Treatment depends on the type of injury, but usually involves putting the affected limb in a cast or splint. Some injuries may also require surgery to repair the damage. Fortunately, about 85 per cent of growth plate injuries heal without any lasting problems, but prompt treatment is essential so children should never be encouraged to exercise if they are in any pain. Left untreated, growth plate injuries can cause permanent damage, so take aches and pains seriously.

Bullying

Bullying can have a huge impact on children – and if it happens in a sporting situation, it can be enough to put them off sports and exercise for good. Most children will experience some gentle teasing every now and again, but name-calling, sarcasm and verbal abuse should never be tolerated.

Most schools and sports clubs are well aware of the effects of bullying: it can destroy a child's confidence and seriously affect their social, emotional and academic development. Bullying can take a number of forms:

- ▶ *Verbal: This involves name-calling or making threats.*
- ▶ *Psychological: This is usually based on spreading rumours and making a child feel excluded or unsafe.*
- ▶ *Physical: This involves pushing, hitting or physically hurting a child.*

Although bullying can begin as early as pre-school, it's more common in primary and secondary school children. In general, girls tend to engage more in verbal or psychological bullying, whereas boys are more likely to start fights or make threats of violence. Bullying can have very serious consequences and can lead to depression, anxiety and low self-esteem, so it should always be taken very seriously by parents, schools and sports clubs.

Unfortunately, bullying doesn't just happen at the hands of other children. In some cases, teachers and coaches can be guilty of deliberately embarrassing, ignoring or verbally abusing a child – often as a way to try to improve their performance.

Some coaches are particularly hard on talented athletes, as a means to push them to succeed, but no child should be forced into rigorous training, competition or put under pressure to perform to unrealistically high standards. Neither should less able children be teased about their lack of ability or forced to practise in extreme heat or cold as a means to 'toughen them up'. Remember, sarcastic comments and constant criticism is a form of abuse, so it's very important to act immediately if your child is distressed.

Insight

Encourage your child to talk to you about their feelings and emotions, particularly those connected to their relationships with others. Bullying thrives on secrecy, so you should find it easier to nip any problems in the bud if the lines of communication are open.

Is your child being bullied?

Sometimes a child won't admit to being bullied, even if you ask them outright. This is usually because they are embarrassed, or scared that their bullying will get worse if they tell a parent or teacher. However, there are some common signs that your child is being bullied that you can look out for. These include:

▶ *depression and/or mood swings*
▶ *frequent headaches or stomach aches*
▶ *asking for time off school due to imaginary or minor illnesses*
▶ *seeming on edge*
▶ *spending more time than usual alone*
▶ *a sudden dislike of school or after-school activities*
▶ *a change in eating habits*
▶ *reports from teachers that they are not performing as well at school*
▶ *avoiding social situations*
▶ *differences in sleep patterns*
▶ *changing the route or method of transport they take to school or sports clubs*
▶ *losing valuable possessions.*

If your child is exhibiting several of these signs, then it may be an indication that they are being bullied. If they won't talk to you about it, then you may want to talk to your child's teacher, coach or a good friend to find out if they are aware of a problem.

HOW TO HELP

If you suspect that your child is being bullied, then you need to work out the best way to put a stop to it. First, persuade your child to tell you what is happening. If they feel that they are being bullied by a teacher or coach, you should go straight to your child's school or sports club and raise your concerns with the headteacher or club leader. If they don't seem to take you seriously, then you may have to make an official complaint and, if possible, organize different classes for your child.

Most cases of bullying occur between groups of children, and this can be tricky to resolve effectively. Depending on the situation, it's best to talk through possible solutions with your child. Sometimes ignoring the bully and staying out of their way can be enough to diffuse the situation. If not, ask a friend or older sibling to keep an eye on your child, as this may help to boost their confidence and keep bullies at bay. Something as simple as coming up with a few responses to the bullies taunts or spiteful comments can often help to boost a child's confidence. In more serious cases, your child will need help to handle the situation, so it's best to have a chat to your child's teacher or coach to ask them to help you put a stop to it. Often teachers are unaware of the problem, and bringing it out into the open can be enough to convince bullies to stop.

In extreme cases, particularly if physical violence is involved, you may need to contact the police. Long-term bullying can have serious, sometimes tragic, consequences, so it's vital to nip it in the bud.

Helping children with health problems to get fit

There's no reason why children with health problems can't get fit and active, so don't let your child use this as an excuse to avoid sport. In fact, some common conditions such as asthma and diabetes can actually be improved by participating in sports, although you must check with your child's doctor before they begin. Provided that your child understands how to handle their condition – for example, using an inhaler for asthma or taking regular insulin injections for diabetes – and their teachers or coach are aware of it too, then it should be safe for them to take part in most sports. The following section gives details of some of the most common childhood health concerns, along with suggestions on the sports that might suit your child the most.

Insight

Don't let your child use their health problems as an excuse to avoid exercise. Many conditions are easier to manage if your child is fit and active so, provided you have the all clear from your GP, encourage your child to get moving.

ASTHMA

Asthma is a condition that affects the airways. When a person with asthma comes into contact with something that irritates their airways – known as a trigger – the muscles around the walls of the airways tighten so that the airways become narrower. The lining of the airways then starts to swell, which makes it harder to breathe. The usual symptoms of asthma are coughing, shortness of breath, wheezing and tightness in the chest. It's not unusual for children to grow out of asthma, and many find that their symptoms become milder as they get older.

Many children with asthma are reluctant to take part in sports. This is sometimes because they find that they become breathless and uncomfortable and this makes them self-conscious – and sometimes because they worry that exercise might bring on an asthma attack. In fact, exercise can be a trigger for some children, but this is usually an indication that their asthma is not very well controlled, so it's a good idea to visit the doctor to review their medication.

Taking part in sport can be hugely beneficial to an asthmatic child, as it increases lung capacity and improves overall fitness.

However, certain activities are better than others. Children with asthma often struggle with sports that demand long periods of activity as this tends to make them breathless. Team sports such as football or hockey are less likely to trigger an attack as they involve brief periods of activity with short breaks in between. Swimming is another good option as the warm, humid air makes breathing easier. Cold, dry air can bring on attack, so try to avoid exercising outdoors in cold weather, and activities such as skiing and ice-skating can also cause problems. If your child is keen to try any of these types of activities, then get advice from your doctor first.

Teach your child what to do if they have an asthma attack, and make sure that they keep their inhaler with them at all times. If exercise triggers your child's asthma, then they should use their reliever inhaler before taking part, and warm up and cool down gradually to minimize the risk of an attack. Check that your child's teachers or coach knows that they suffer from asthma – and leave a spare inhaler with your child's name on it at their school or sports club, just in case they forget to take their own.

> Did you know?
> According to Asthma UK, over 1.1 million children in the UK (that's one in ten children) are currently receiving treatment for asthma.

DIABETES

Diabetes is a condition in which the amount of glucose (sugar) in the blood is too high because the body does not produce enough of the hormone insulin to process it. Type 1 diabetes occurs when the body cannot make any insulin; type 2 diabetes occurs when the body cannot make enough, or when the insulin it produces doesn't work properly. Type 1 diabetes is the least common of the two types. It usually occurs before the age of 40 and requires insulin injections or medications. Type 2 diabetes is linked with being overweight and is most commonly seen in people over the age of 40. However, recently more children – some as young as seven – are being diagnosed with type 2 diabetes, usually as a result of being overweight. Type 2 diabetes can often be controlled by losing weight, eating healthily and taking more exercise.

Managing diabetes requires careful monitoring of diet, exercise and medication to keep blood glucose levels as close to normal as possible. The main risk of exercise for children with diabetes is hypoglycaemia, also known as having a 'hypo'. This happens when blood sugar levels drop too low, and if it is not treated your child could become confused, sleepy or even lose consciousness.

Hypoglycaemia usually occurs as a result of one or more of the following: too much insulin, not enough food, too much exercise, a delayed meal, stress or time in hot weather. Common symptoms include hunger, shaking, wobbly legs, butterflies in the tummy, sweating, dizziness and blurred vision. The best way to treat a hypo is to give your child a sugary snack, followed by a sandwich or carbohydrate-rich snack. This usually solves the problem, so make sure that your child carries an emergency snack and that their teacher or coach knows what to do if they have a hypo. This aside, the benefits of taking exercise greatly outweigh the risks provided you follow a few simple guidelines.

▶ *Ask your doctor how to manage your child's glucose levels when they are exercising.*
▶ *Try to ensure that your child exercises at the same time every day.*
▶ *Encourage your child to exercise soon after eating, when blood sugar levels are highest.*
▶ *Ask your child to check their blood sugar levels before exercising.*
▶ *Encourage your child to carry a sugary or carbohydrate snack with them when exercising.*
▶ *Don't inject insulin into a part of the body that is being exercised, as this will result in it being absorbed too quickly.*
▶ *Make sure that your child wears ID saying that they have diabetes.*
▶ *Make sure that your child's teachers or coach know what to do in the event of an emergency.*

Unless your doctor tells you otherwise, children with diabetes can take part in any sport. However it's a good idea to start slowly and increase fitness gradually as this gives you plenty of time to monitor the effects on your child's blood sugar levels.

ADHD

Attention Deficit Hyperactivity Disorder (ADHD), sometimes called Attention Deficit Disorder (ADD), is the most common childhood behavioural disorder. It affects 5 per cent of children in the UK and is caused by a chemical imbalance that causes the brain to have problems processing all the information it receives. ADHD can be hereditary, and symptoms usually start around the age of four. Different children have different symptoms, but these can include:

▶ *poor concentration*
▶ *restless behaviour*
▶ *little sense of danger*
▶ *difficulty following instructions*
▶ *finding it hard to wait their turn*
▶ *interrupting others*
▶ *having little control over what they say and do.*

In addition to these symptoms, ADHD may also have an impact on speech, language and coordination. As sufferers are usually bursting with energy, many parents assume that they will enjoy sports. However, many children with ADHD run into problems because they find it hard to follow instructions and have a tendency to take risks that may put themselves or other children in danger.

Despite this, children with ADHD can really benefit from sporting activities – providing they have the right instruction. When taught properly, sports can improve their social skills, teach them to work as part of a team and help them to make friends more easily. It can also improve coordination and increase self-confidence – so it really is worth finding a sport or activity that your child can enjoy.

Before you begin, make sure that your child's teacher or coach understands their condition and is able to supervise them very closely to ensure that they don't put themselves or others at risk. For this reason, you may find that it's best to start with individual sports such as swimming, dancing or martial arts, as this gives your child opportunity to learn at their own pace, without being thrown into a team environment that may make them uncomfortable. If your child takes prescribed medication for their condition, you may also want to check with your doctor to find out if the dosage needs to be adjusted.

Sports and activities for children with disabilities

Taking part in sports and physical activities can benefit children with disabilities in many ways. It can strengthen muscles, improve joint mobility, improve balance and coordination and increase self-confidence. If you are keen to introduce your child to organized sports, then think about the type of activities that would suit your child best – and how they would most like to get involved.

There are many different types of sports clubs that disabled children can join, and these offer several different types of sporting experience. Some children will be happier in a single impairment club, where they know that all activities will be arranged with their particular disability in mind. For example, Actionnaires clubs, organized by Action For Blind People give children who are blind or have a visual impairment the opportunity to participate in sports outside of school in a safe, structured and fun environment. Similarly, Mencap runs sports clubs for children with learning disabilities, providing the opportunity for their members to get and keep fit.

Some sports clubs and groups offer sports and activities to children with a wide range of disabilities: these types of clubs are often run by local charities. There are also sports clubs that specialize in a particular sport – such as goalball (for visually impaired people), boccia (for people with cerebral palsy and other disabilities affecting motor skills) and wheelchair basketball, all of which are recognized Paralympic sports.

It's important to recognize that some disabled children will prefer to take part in sports in the same way that non-disabled children do. This means that they may want to join the nearest sports club that offers their chosen activity. Sports clubs should be inclusive and open to a disabled person joining, although make sure that the staff understand your child's disability and have the time and patience to give them the attention they need to fulfil their sporting potential.

Disability sports organizations can give you lots of information on the best way to get started, and the Youth Sports Trust has designed a programme called TOP Sportsability, which is designed to encourage young people with disabilities to enjoy participating in PE and sport.

Once your child finds a sport that they enjoy, do all you can to encourage their interest and praise their achievements, even if they seem to be making very slow progress. It's important to help your child to set their own goals and not compare themselves to other children. This way they can enjoy a great deal of personal satisfaction and a whole new understanding of their own capabilities.

SPORTS FOR CHILDREN WITH AUTISTIC SPECTRUM DISORDER

Autistic Spectrum Disorder is the term that is used to describe a group of disorders, including Autism and Asperger Syndrome. Autistic Spectrum Disorder (ASD) is a lifelong condition that affects social interaction and communication. Research suggest that about 1 in 100 people have ASD in the UK, and it affects four times as many boys as girls. The causes of ASD are still unknown, and there is no cure, however, treatments are available.

A child with ASD may find it hard to relate to other people and have trouble understanding their own or other people's emotions. They may also have problems with speech and language, find it difficult to understand gestures, facial expressions and tones of voice and may struggle to follow instructions. Children may also have a tendency to play the same games over and over again, and get very upset if their routine is disrupted. Children with Asperger Syndrome generally have fewer problems with language but still experience difficulty with social interaction.

Although children with ASD can be hard to motivate and resistant to exercise, experts now believe that sport can be very beneficial. Not only can it help to reduce repetitive behaviour, but it can also improve social interaction. Many children with ASD will struggle with team sports, but it's not usually their physical skills that hold them back, it's their social skills. For this reason, they are much more suited to individual sports such as swimming, golf, martial arts or running as this doesn't involve close interaction with other children.

Depending on the severity of your child's condition, they may be able to join a regular sports club or class. If you feel that your child needs some extra help and support, then perhaps you should think about one-to-one tuition, or you could look for a teacher who has some experience of teaching children with ASD. Whatever you decide, make sure that the coach or instructor knows about your child's ASD and is prepared to work with them to get the best result.

Did you know?

Up to half of children with ASD are prescribed drugs that can cause swift weight gain. Studies show that about 17 per cent of children with ASD are overweight and about 35 per cent are at risk of becoming overweight, so encouraging a child with ASD to take regular exercise is a great way to reduce the risk of obesity and weight-related illness in later life.

Sports and activities for children with Asperger Syndrome

Individual sports are best for Stuart, as he doesn't connect as part of a team and often plays alongside, rather than with, other children. He also copes best with sports that don't involve a lot of repetition. He gave up kung fu because he was frustrated with repeating the same movements every week, and although he is good at swimming, he has given up structured lessons, for the same reason. He seems to think he should be able to do things without practising, and he can't share his feelings so it's hard to know whether he's enjoying something or not.

Since he started at a mainstream school, we have had some problems with PE. Stuart struggles if it gets too noisy or if he finds a particular activity difficult, has trouble following vague or complicated instructions and tends to get bored or angry when things don't go his way. For these reasons he prefers disability sport, because he enjoys playing with other children like him. However, as we live in a small town our options are fairly limited, and it can be hard to find groups that have instructors with the patience and understanding he needs.

Despite all these setbacks, it's been well worth getting Stuart involved in sports. He still needs lots of encouragement to take part – usually the promise of more time on the Xbox – as his social problems make it hard for him, but sport has boosted his confidence, and improved his social skills and understanding of teamwork. He has also developed a personal sense of achievement and pride, which helps him in the classroom, and also when he's playing with other children.

Sharon is mum to Stuart, eight, who has Asperger Syndrome.

10 THINGS TO REMEMBER

1 *Children are more accident prone than adults, so it's important to use the recommended safety equipment at all times.*

2 *Children should always be supervised when playing sports.*

3 *It's important to teach your child to warm up and cool down before and after exercise.*

4 *Head injuries should always be taken seriously, particularly if your child loses consciousness.*

5 *Seek medical attention if bleeding from a cut does not stop within ten minutes.*

6 *Treat sprains and strains with the RICE method (Rest, Ice, Compression, Elevation).*

7 *If you suspect that your child is being bullied, raise your concerns with their sports teacher or coach.*

8 *If your child has health issues, make sure that they and their sports teacher/coach know how to manage their condition and what to do in an emergency.*

9 *Some disabled children prefer to join a club with non-disabled children, while others prefer clubs that are geared to their particular disability. Don't make assumptions – ask your child which they prefer.*

10 *Regular exercise can help to counteract the weight gain that is associated with the drugs prescribed to manage ASD.*

10

Overweight children

In this chapter you will learn:
- *how to determine if your child is overweight*
- *how to help your child maintain a healthy weight*
- *how to help your overweight child to get fit.*

It can be difficult to tell if a growing child is overweight – and some parents don't like to admit, even to themselves, that their child is carrying a few extra pounds. This is often because they believe that any excess weight is just 'puppy fat' that their child will grow out of. Or sometimes they think that their child is 'big boned' – a very common assumption, especially if the whole family is overweight.

It doesn't help that there is so much guilt and shame attached to obesity, particularly where children are concerned. Parents who have a weight problem themselves tend to worry that they are to blame if their child is overweight. Equally, parents who are naturally slim sometimes feel confused and embarrassed if their child is overweight or obese. They often feel guilty that they have allowed it to happen, and are so worried about upsetting their child by discussing the subject that they find it difficult to make any changes.

> ### Did you know?
> According to the Foresight report, the rise in childhood obesity will have a huge impact on our children's health as

they reach middle age. Unless we act now, the report predicts that by 2050:

- ▶ *60 per cent of men will be obese*
- ▶ *50 per cent of women will be obese*
- ▶ *26 per cent of children will be obese*
- ▶ *cases of type 2 diabetes will rise by 70 per cent*
- ▶ *cases of stroke will rise by 30 per cent*
- ▶ *cases of coronary heart disease will rise by 20 per cent.*

Your role as a parent

The first thing to understand is that feeling guilty won't help you to help your child. In fact, it may have quite the opposite effect. If you blame yourself for your child's weight problem, then it's possible that you may inadvertently make the situation worse by indulging your child and allowing them to eat unhealthy foods or spend too much time in front of the television, purely because you want to make them happy.

What your child really needs is for you to take control of the situation and help them to achieve a healthy weight. In order to do this, you will need to think about the reasons why they gained weight in the first place. You will find information on how to do this later in the chapter.

Insight

You might not be able to influence how your child eats when you're not around, but you can control what they eat at home. If you stop buying chocolates, crisps and biscuits, then your child can't eat them – it's as simple as that! That's not to say you can't buy them the occasional bar or chocolate, packet of crisps or ice cream as a treat, but buying single servings and avoid multi-packs or buy-one-get-one-free offers. This makes portion control much easier.

Of course, you must be prepared to meet with some resistance from your child – but stick to your guns because the results will be worth it. To boost your motivation, think hard about all the reasons why it's important for your child to be a healthy weight. Remind yourself of health risks associated with childhood obesity, which are outlined in Chapter 1. And remember that the social and emotional consequences of being overweight will multiply as your child gets older – for example, an overweight child is more likely to be teased or bullied and is likely to feel increasingly self-conscious about their body as they reach puberty.

The good news is that there are several reasons why it's easier for children to lose, or control, their weight than it is for adults:

▶ *Children are still growing, so they naturally burn off more calories than adults.*
▶ *Young children are naturally active, so you can boost their activity levels simply by encouraging active play.*
▶ *To a great extent, you can make healthy choices for your children. If you decide to prepare healthy meals and refuse to buy fizzy drinks, sugary snacks and junk food, even the most resistant child will begin to eat more healthily.*

Most importantly, remember that everyone in the family will benefit from eating a healthy diet and taking more exercise, so don't feel that you have to single your child out or put them on a strict diet because this would probably do more harm than good. Later in this chapter you will learn how making a series of small changes is the key to success. But before we go any further, it's a good idea to establish whether your child's weight is a cause for concern.

Did you know?
According to Professor Paul Gately, director of Carnegie Weight Management at Leeds Metropolitan University, eight out of ten obese children will become obese adults.

Is your child overweight?

If you suspect that your child is overweight, then you must acknowledge the problem and work out the best way to address it. The sooner you do this the better, as it's much easier to help a young child who isn't yet old enough to go to the shops and buy unhealthy snacks when you're not around.

There are several methods that can help you decide whether or not your child is overweight. First, when your child is undressed, look for any soft rolls of flesh around their tummy, under their chin, or on their upper arms or legs. If any are visible, then it's an indication that their body fat ratio may be a little too high.

BODY MASS INDEX

Instead of simply weighing your child, work out their Body Mass Index (BMI) as this also takes your child's height into account. To do this you will first need to measure your child's weight in kilograms and their height in metres. Then use the following formula to calculate your child's BMI:

$$\frac{\text{Weight in kilograms}}{\text{Height in metres} \times \text{Height in metres}} = \text{BMI}$$

So grab a calculator and multiply your child's height in metres by itself. Then divide your child's weight in kilograms by this number. The resulting figure is your child's BMI.

You can now plot your child's BMI on to the graphs that you'll find in Appendix I. There is a separate chart for boys and for girls, so find your child's age across the bottom of the relevant chart, and their BMI in the column that runs up the side. If your child's BMI falls into the shaded area on the chart, then your child is within the healthy weight range. If your child's BMI falls above the first heavy black line, then they may be overweight; if you child's BMI falls above the second heavy black line, then they could be obese.

Remember that BMI charts like this should only be used as a helpful guide, as they don't always give the full picture. For instance, when measuring your child's weight, it's impossible to distinguish between body fat and muscle mass. So a perfectly healthy, but rather muscular, child may have a high BMI, even though they are not overweight. Similarly, a child who has a poor diet and doesn't get much exercise may fall into the healthy range, even though they are at risk of gaining weight unless they change their habits.

It's also perfectly normal to notice rapid changes in BMI during growth spurts. For this reason, the best way to monitor your child's weight is to check their BMI every six months and mark it on the chart. This will help you to track any slow but steady increases, or decreases in weight, which should help you to nip any potential weight problems in the bud.

WAIST CIRCUMFERENCE

Because your child's BMI doesn't always tell the full story, it's a good idea to also measure your child's waist circumference. Simply take a tape measure and measure around your child's waist, midway between the bottom of the ribs and the hips, just as your child finishes breathing out. Take the measurement in centimetres, then plot it on the relevant waist circumference chart in Appendix II – bearing in mind that there is a separate chart for boys and girls. Again, find your child's age across the bottom of the chart and their waist measurement in centimetres, which runs up the side of the chart. If your child falls within the shaded area, they are within the healthy range. If they fall above this range, they have a high waist circumference measurement which, taken along with a high BMI, indicates that they are very probably overweight. If their weight falls above the second broken line, they are likely to be obese.

Even if your child's BMI reading and waist measurement do fall outside the healthy range, then it's important not to panic. Following the healthy lifestyle changes set out in this book can only be beneficial to you and your family, but you should never put your child on a strict diet or exercise regime. If these tests indicate that you have reason to be concerned about your child's weight, then consult your doctor to confirm that your child is indeed overweight, and discuss the best way to proceed.

'I didn't realize that my child was overweight.'

Amelia was a large baby – she weighed over ten pounds when she was born – and grew into a larger-than-average toddler. She has always had a healthy diet, and has never been allowed to eat junk food, so it never occurred to me that her weight could be an issue. It wasn't until Amelia joined a ballet class when she was three, that I noticed how much bigger she was than all the other girls who looked tiny in their leotards in comparison.

I had a word with our health visitor, who confirmed that Amelia was overweight, and explained that although she eats very healthily, she was eating too much – and not getting enough exercise to burn it off. Since then we have reduced Amelia's portion sizes. We've done it gradually so she hasn't really noticed, and have bought her some smaller plates, which help to limit the amount of food she can eat at mealtimes. We've also made more of an effort to keep active, and we now go to the playground most days and play lots of active games at home.

We felt terribly guilty when we realized that we were setting Amelia up for a weight problem, but we're fortunate that we've been able to nip it in the bud. Her weight gain has

*now slowed right down and we're confident that she'll fit
into the healthy range before she starts school.*

Justine is mum to Amelia, four.

> ### Did you know?
> Statistics show that 70 per cent of parents with overweight
> children think that they are a normal weight, while 30 per cent
> of parents with obese children think that their children are
> 'just right'.

IF YOUR CHILD IS UNDERWEIGHT

If your child's weight and BMI indicates that they are underweight,
then it's important to consult your doctor. Bear in mind that it's
not unusual for growing children to go through periods of being
underweight, and it's usually because they are so active that they
are burning up more calories than they are eating. This is also
fairly common among fussy eaters, who will eat only a limited
variety of foods.

If your child is underweight, then it's important to ensure that
they are eating a healthy, balanced diet containing foods from
every food group. Resist the temptation to allow them to fill up
on unhealthy, high-calorie junk foods – these foods are not at all
nutritious or healthy and even if your child is underweight they
should only be eaten as an occasional treat.

Instead, try to make sure that your child eats little and often.
Make sure that they eat three meals each day and encourage them
to eat a little more at every mealtime – for example, an extra slice
of toast at breakfast or an extra potato at dinner. Provide healthy
snacks such as fruit, nuts, yoghurt or chunks of cheese for them to
eat between meals.

Provided that your doctor rules out any underlying health issues,
there is no reason why your child should stop exercising, even if
they are underweight – just make sure that they are eating enough
to keep them going.

Finally, keep an eye on children – particularly boys – who are small for their age as they approach puberty. Many pre-teen boys worry about being underweight, and so begin intense exercise regimes and weight training in an effort to bulk up. This kind of workout isn't suitable for children as it places their bodies under too much strain. If you suspect that your child is trying to build muscle, ask their PE teacher to keep an eye on them and suggest some safer alternatives.

Tackling your child's weight problem

If your child is overweight or obese, you should never put them on a weight loss diet unless supervised by your doctor. Restricting a child's food intake can affect their growth, and it could also put your child at risk of developing serious eating disorders such as anorexia or bulimia. Weight loss programmes designed for adults – particularly those that involve meal replacements or promise fast weight loss – are never suitable for children, and should be avoided at all costs.

Unless your child has severe weight-related health problems, most experts believe that the best approach is to reduce your child's BMI over a period of time by:

▶ *working to slow the rate of weight gain*
or
▶ *working to stop the weight gain.*

This is usually the most appropriate solution for children because it allows them to 'grow into' their weight as they get taller. Consequently, you should not expect to get results overnight – after all, it takes time to gain weight and it takes time to lose it too. The key is to make a series of small improvements to your child's diet, while increasing their activity levels. This should help you to establish a healthier lifestyle that will benefit your family's health for years to come.

The best way to get your child's weight under control is to focus
on healthy eating, which is explained in more detail in the following
chapter. You will probably need to make some lifestyle changes
too, but this doesn't need to be a daunting task.

POSSIBLE REASONS FOR A WEIGHT INCREASE

First, you will need to consider the reasons why your child became
overweight in the first place. The following statements represent
some of the most common reasons why children gain weight.
Once you identify which ones apply to you and your family, read
through the tips and suggestions detailed below each statement and
you will be in a good position to make changes.

I use food to reward or comfort my child
Many parents use food to reward or comfort their child. If you are
aware that you do this, then it's important to stop – now. There
are lots of other ways to show your love. A kiss and a cuddle
should be enough to comfort an upset child, so there's really no
need to use food. If you want to reward your child, then think
about activities that they enjoy – perhaps allow them to invite a
friend round to play, plan a fun day out or allow them to watch
a favourite television programme instead.

> **Insight**
>
> Comforting your child with food is such a natural and
> automatic response that it can be tough to break. Don't

worry if you do it from time to time, but try not to use
sugary treats as a way to bribe your child, as it can easily
become a habit. If you must, think about offering healthier
treats instead – home-made ice lollies, frozen yoghurt or a
smoothie all fit the bill.

I find it hard to deny my child their favourite – unhealthy – foods
It's not unusual for children to favour unhealthy foods. Pizza,
chips, burgers, cakes, chocolate and ice cream are all favourites –
and all of them are packed with calories and unhealthy fats and
have little nutritional value. However, your child can still enjoy
these items, provided you adapt them to fit in with your new
healthy eating regime.

Instead of fried chips, make oven-baked potato, or sweet potato
wedges. They are quick and easy to make, and if you toss them in
olive oil before baking they are much healthier than conventional
chips. Make your own pizza using pitta bread as a base, and top
with sweetcorn, mushrooms and any other vegetables that your
child enjoys. Make your own ice lollies using fresh fruit and
yoghurt. Simply pour the mixture into ice-lolly moulds and keep
a few in the freezer. You can make your own burgers out of lean
beef mince and instead of shop-bought cakes consider making
your own. It's easy to find recipes for healthy banana muffins or
flapjacks that are much lower in fat and sugar than the ones you
find in shops. Make a batch and store them in the freezer so that
they are ready when you need them.

If your child enjoys chocolate, crisps and biscuits, then there's no
need to ban them completely. But try to avoid keeping them in the
house – instead buy your child a small, single-serving packet every
once in a while. Buying large bars of chocolates or multi-packs
makes it hard to keep an eye on how much your child is eating –
and if your child knows that you have these snacks in the house,
then they are likely to pester you until you give in – or simply help
themselves.

My child eats similar-sized portions to the rest of the family

Parents often overestimate quite how much food their child needs – and some young children will routinely eat an adult-size portion. Studies show that the more children are served, the more they are likely to eat – so it's best to avoid putting too much food on your child's plate, or even using smaller plates.

You may also find it helpful to think in terms of the amount of calories your child needs every day. The following table should give you an idea of what to aim for, bearing in mind that very active children may need more, and those that are quite inactive may need less:

Age	Calories per day	
	Boys	Girls
Age 1–3	1,200	1,165
Age 4–6	1,700	1,550
Age 7–10	1,950	1,750
Age 11–14	2,200	1,850

If you suspect that your child is eating too much, then keep a food diary for a few days, and write down everything that they eat and drink. You can then use a calorie counter, which you can buy quite cheaply at most good bookshops, to calculate how many calories your child consumes on a typical day. If they consume more than the recommended amount, then you may need to think about reducing portion size and/or increasing their activity levels so that they burn off more energy.

Insight

Buying your child their own plate, bowl and cutlery can really help you to control portion sizes. Look for plates decorated with your child's favourite television characters or let them chose designs that they like best. Look for a plate that's roughly the size of a side plate, and fill it sensibly – don't pile it high. Encourage your child to eat slowly and wait for at least 15 minutes to check that they really are hungry before they have a second helping.

My child prefers fizzy drinks to water or juice

The best drinks for your child are milk or water. Sugary drinks can damage your children's teeth, and contribute to weight gain if they are consumed regularly. Even fruit juice is full of natural sugar, so it's best to dilute this with water and keep it to a minimum if your child is overweight. If your child likes fizzy drinks, then consider diluting orange or apple juice with sparkling water and ice instead.

My child is a fussy eater

Many parents worry about how to feed a fussy eater – and some children will only agree to eat a very limited variety of, usually unhealthy, foods. Unfortunately, there is no easy solution here. Remember that you are doing your child no favours by allowing them to eat unhealthy foods, so try to introduce healthier options that your child might find appealing. Younger children often respond well to individual portions – such as mini pies made in ramekin dishes or bite-sized fishcakes. You could also use cookie cutters to make shaped sandwiches. Choose from stars, hearts, animals – or even spell out your child's name or initials.

Don't be afraid to try a few gimmicks, either. Cook a stir-fry and encourage the whole family to eat with chopsticks. Or prepare some chilli, strips of grilled meat and mashed avocado with tortillas, so that everyone can roll up their own Mexican-style fajitas. Some parents find that asking their child to help in preparing healthy meals is enough to build their enthusiasm. If that doesn't work, then think about inviting your child's friends round for tea. Watching other children eat healthy food can often work wonders for children, as they are usually keen to fit in and do what their friends do. Usually some of these techniques will tempt even the fussiest eaters.

Insight

Provided that your child's favourite foods aren't too unhealthy, don't worry about them eating a repetitive diet. It's not unusual for young children to want to eat the same things day in day out and they will grow out of this eventually. In the meantime,

(Contd)

offer subtle variations to their tried-and-tested favourites, introduce a new food once per week and let them try things from your plate.

My child doesn't like fruit and vegetables
If your child refuses to eat fruit and vegetables, you may need to learn to disguise them. Add extra carrots, peppers and mushrooms when you are making a tomato sauce for pasta – if you blend this down to a smooth consistency they are unlikely to notice the difference. If your child will eat mashed potato, then think about mixing this with some mashed cauliflower. Using a julienne peeler to slice vegetables into strings is a great way to encourage children to eat carrots, courgettes or squash – and can be easily mixed in with spaghetti. Mini vegetables are also quite appealing to children – so try introducing babycorn, cherry tomatoes or baby courgettes. If your child isn't keen on fruit, then mix up a smoothie using a handful of fruit, half a banana, milk and yoghurt. Sweeten it with a little honey if necessary and call it a milkshake!

My child usually snacks in front of the television
Studies show that eating in front of the television has a direct link to obesity. This is partly because the type of foods that children tend to eat in this situation are fatty, sugary, high-calorie snacks such as crisps, chocolate, biscuits, chips or pizza. The best option is to ban eating in front of the television. But if this isn't workable for you, then at the very least you should provide healthier snacks for your children to eat instead. Chunks of fruit, pitta bread with hummus, nuts, dried fruits, or even a bowl of breakfast cereal are all healthier options that will help to keep your child's weight under control.

My child doesn't take regular exercise
Turn back to Chapters 1 and 2 to remind yourself of the reasons why you should keep your child fit and active. If your child's weight makes exercise difficult, then you will find more suggestions on how to get started towards the end of this chapter.

We rarely eat together as a family

Regular family mealtimes are one of the best ways to keep an eye on what your child is eating, and establish good habits that will last for a lifetime. If you can, aim to eat together at least once a day. Structured mealtimes not only help your child to eat a balanced diet and reduce the likelihood that they will need to snack between meals, but also discourage the whole family from eating on the run and relying too heavily on junk food and takeaways. If you are to tackle your child's health problem successfully, it's advisable to take a family approach. Giving your child different foods to the rest of the family will single them out and make them feel resentful and excluded. Putting your child under pressure to make big changes to their diet and lifestyle can make them feel that they are being punished for being overweight – so take it slowly, and get the whole family involved.

My child doesn't eat breakfast

It's important to get your child into the habit of eating breakfast every morning. If they don't, they are much more likely to eat unhealthy snacks such as crisps and chocolate by mid-morning – and their performance at school could suffer too. Studies have shown that children who eat breakfast have improved concentration levels, are more alert and are even better behaved – so tempt your child with healthy cereal such as porridge or wheat biscuits, wholegrain toast, eggs, fruit or yoghurt. Try to avoid unhealthy options such as sugary breakfast cereals, breakfast bars, pastries or muffins as these are high in calories and won't keep your child full until lunch.

Insight

Don't feel that you can only offer your child traditional breakfast foods. You could make 'breakfast pizzas' from crumpets or pittas topped with cheese, tomato and ham, a cheese or ham sandwich or beans on toast. Many children dislike cereal and eggs, and mornings will become very stressful if you try to push these on your child.

Case study: Cutting out junk food

The problem

James is an 11-year-old boy who refuses to eat healthy food. He has BMI of 26, which means that James is obese. His weight problem has got steadily worse through his childhood and there is a history of obesity in his family. James's love of junk food is at the root of his weight problem. Despite his parents' best efforts, he refuses to eat 'healthy' food and snacks on chocolate, crisps and fizzy drinks and often buys chips on his way home from school.

The solution

Instead of trying to persuade James to eat meals that he doesn't recognize, his parents, Claire and Pete, decided to try a new approach. They asked James what he would like to eat if it was up to him, and he chose southern fried chicken, sausages and mash, burgers, chips and pizza. James's mum then looked for recipes that explained how to cook healthy versions of these foods and found that James was much more willing to eat them. His favourite meals now include home-made burgers in a wholemeal bun with low fat cheese and oven chips, oven-baked crispy chicken with corn on the cob, and pizza made with shop-bought bases, topped with vegetables, wafer-thin ham and reduced fat cheese. Sausages and burgers are grilled rather than fried, and he starts the day with scrambled eggs or beans on toast to keep him going until lunch.

The outcome

Now that he knows he has a tasty dinner to look forward to, James has stopped buying chips on the way home, and eats a proper meal instead. He still has school dinners and sometimes eats takeaway food with his friends, so nobody teases him about being on a diet, but the rest of his diet is so much improved that he is steadily losing weight.

Weight loss camps

Weight loss camps, commonly known as 'Fat Camps', have been popular in the US for some time. They are now gaining in popularity in the UK, with the Carnegie Weight Management Camps, developed at Leeds Metropolitan University, leading the way. The residential camps are open to eight- to seventeen-year-olds who are overweight or obese, with a minimum two-week stay. For children who don't want to stay away from home, day camps and weekend or after-school clubs are also available. The camps offer guaranteed results without resorting to a boot-camp approach or putting children on strict diets. Instead, children are given the opportunity to try lots of physical activities and are taught about healthy eating and good food choices. The social aspect is also very important, as children are given lots of time to make friends with other campers.

If you think that a weight loss camp could help your child, then do your homework before you commit. If you are considering a residential camp, make sure that you are happy with the regime that your child will be following, and that the programme is designed and run by qualified professionals. Weight loss camps can be very costly, so you should always ask to see published results of the programme to make sure that you're not wasting your money. It's also a good idea to check that the camp offers some follow-up support so that your child doesn't slip back into their old habits as soon as they return home.

Before you commit to a residential camp, consider how your child will cope with staying away from home for a period of time. You should also make sure that your child actually wants to make changes and sees camp as a positive experience – if they are pushed into going against their wishes, it's unlikely they will put their best efforts into maintaining the programme and will probably regard their enrolment as a form of punishment for being overweight. This will do nothing to boost their self-esteem and may serve to make their problem worse.

Exercise for overweight children

If your child is overweight, there is every chance that they are not getting the recommended amount of exercise each day. It could be that they have gained weight as a result of not getting enough exercise – or perhaps they find exercise uncomfortable or embarrassing as a result of their excess weight. There is evidence to suggest that lack of exercise actually follows weight gain, rather than causes it – but whichever way you look at it, it's important to break the cycle and help your child to get fit.

Children who are overweight are often reluctant to take part in traditional forms of exercise, usually because they are worried about being teased by other children, either because their weight affects their performance or because they quickly get hot, sweaty and breathless. Older children often become embarrassed about their bodies, too – so they worry about getting changed in front of other children or wearing sports kit.

In order to help your child get active, it's a good idea to start small. Try to encourage them to walk every day, and think about activities that you can enjoy as a family, as outlined in Chapter 3. This is a great way to motivate your child to increase the amount of exercise they take, without feeling that they are being singled out just because they are overweight.

Don't let concerns about your child's size or fitness put you off organized sports. However, it's not a good idea to push your child into competitive team sports or high-impact activities, such as running. These can be daunting for children who are unfit, and will only serve to convince your child that they are not cut out for sport or exercise. Instead, think about individual activities such as swimming – which is a great form of exercise for bigger children – or skill-based activities such as golf, martial arts, archery or fencing. All of these are accessible to children who aren't especially fit and, as most of them require your child to learn and develop a new set of skills, can be a great way to set and achieve personal goals and see steady improvement.

If your child feels too self-conscious to exercise in public, then you could try to tempt them with the promise of new sportswear that they can choose themselves. The thought of a new pair of trainers that they can show off to their friends may be a great incentive to get your child active. If all else fails, think of ways that your child can get active at home. It's possible to pick up second-hand exercise equipment, such as a stationary bike or mini trampoline, fairly cheaply. Encourage your child to play their favourite music and exercise for the duration of two or three 'songs' per session. This way you can steadily build up the amount of time they spend exercising, until their fitness improves to the extent that they feel more comfortable exercising outside the home.

Safe exercise for overweight children

If your child is overweight and unfit, it's a good idea to consult your doctor before you begin an exercise programme. Also bear in mind that overweight and unfit children need to take a little more care when exercising, to reduce the risk of injury. So make sure your child sticks to the following three golden rules:

1 *Warm up and cool down properly. Overweight and unfit children are at greater risk of injury, including muscles strains and joint problems, so they should always take extra time to stretch before and after exercise.*
2 *Bigger children are also likely to sweat more, so encourage your child to drink lots of water when exercising to reduce the risk of dehydration.*
3 *If your child feels sick, dizzy or unwell they should stop exercising immediately.*

Did you know?
BMA research shows that one-third of children aged between two and eleven are taking less than 60 minutes of exercise daily. It is possible that the increasing rates of childhood obesity are to be found in this group of inactive children.

Case study: Helping overweight children to get fit

The problem

Luke is a ten-year-old boy who is self-conscious about exercising because he is significantly overweight. This makes it hard for him to exercise as he gets out of breath very quickly and often has to stop for a rest. Other children tease him because he is overweight, and he worries about getting changed for PE lessons because he doesn't like other children seeing him undress. His parents are monitoring his eating habits to help him lose weight, but are aware that he needs to take more exercise too.

The solution

Luke's parents talked to his PE teacher who agreed to keep an eye on Luke and encourage his efforts to get fit. He also recommended that Luke's parents should find ways to improve his fitness at home, where he would feel less self-conscious. As Luke loves gadgets, his parents bought him a pedometer so that he could monitor how many steps he was taking each day. This worked well because it enabled Luke to set his own goals and, as he gradually increased the amount of steps he was taking, he had a real sense of achievement.

The outcome

Luke's fitness has significantly improved and he is on the way to reaching a healthy weight. He now walks to school every day, and he goes on walks with this family every weekend. Now that he has lost some weight he has also started going swimming, which shows how much his confidence has grown.

10 THINGS TO REMEMBER

1   *You can usually tell by looking if your child has a weight problem, so stop making excuses and be honest with yourself about your child's weight.*

2   *Calculating your child's BMI and measuring their waist circumference will help you to determine if they are a healthy weight.*

3   *The consequences of being overweight will multiply as your child gets older, so it's important to act now.*

4   *Even if your child is overweight, you should not put them on a diet unless your doctor tells you to.*

5   *The best way to tackle your child's weight problem is to slow or stop weight gain so that they can 'grow into' their weight.*

6   *Don't keep unhealthy snack foods such as crisps and biscuits in the house.*

7   *Children need less food than adults, so keep an eye on portion size.*

8   *Eating together as a family can help to establish good eating habits and reduce the urge to snack.*

9   *Eating breakfast will boost your child's concentration, improve their behaviour and make them less likely to crave sugary snacks before lunch.*

10 *Individual activities such as swimming, golf or even using an exercise bike at home are great ways for overweight children to improve their fitness.*

11

Nutrition

In this chapter you will learn:
- *why it's important for your child to eat healthily*
- *how to make changes to your child's diet*
- *which foods you should restrict or avoid.*

There are so many guidelines about what we should and shouldn't eat that it's no wonder we worry about what to feed our children. To add to the confusion, children's nutritional requirements vary according to age, weight and activity – which makes it even harder to determine whether or not they are eating a balanced diet.

It doesn't help that the way we eat has changed significantly since we were children ourselves. The advent of convenience foods has made it quicker and easier to prepare a meal, and many busy families prefer to heat up a ready meal than rush to cook a meal from scratch – and some of us don't really know how to cook because we've never needed to learn. We also tend to eat out more regularly and indulge in high-calorie takeaways – which means that we have become accustomed to large portion sizes and now expect to see much more food on our plates.

Although eating in this way saves time, it isn't good for our waistlines or our overall health, and it's potentially disastrous for our children. One of the best things you can do for your child is teach them how to eat well – and the sooner you start the better, because babies and toddlers who are introduced to a wide range of healthy foods are much more likely to grow up to be healthy eaters.

Encouraging new habits

It's never too late to change your family's eating habits, although you are more likely to meet with some resistance from older children who have already acquired a taste for junk food. But if you've already tried – and failed – to introduce your child to healthy foods, then don't give up, as perseverance usually pays off in the end. None of us find it easy to deny our children the foods they enjoy, but you are not helping your child by allowing them to eat an unhealthy diet. After all, eating a balanced diet will not only help your child to maintain a healthy weight, it will also give them the energy they need to get fit and active. The foods your child eats can also affect the way they feel and the way they behave – so making some positive changes to your child's diet could improve their mood, general behaviour and even their academic performance.

Insight
At first, don't worry about radically changing the way your family eats. Make small changes: buy semi-skimmed milk and reduced-fat cheese instead of full fat, swap white bread, pasta or rice for brown, eat one extra serving of fruit or vegetables each day. Over time, these changes will steadily improve the quality of your diet without anyone feeling deprived.

Fortunately, you don't need to be a whiz in the kitchen to plan and prepare healthy meals for the whole family. Once you understand the basic principles of good nutrition, you will find that eating healthily doesn't have to be complicated, boring, expensive or time-consuming – and there's no need to give up all your favourite foods.

Variety is the cornerstone of good nutrition – eating too much of one thing, especially high-fat or high-sugar foods, means that your child won't get the broad range of nutrients that make up a balanced diet. Provided that your child eats a variety of foods, it won't matter if they have the occasional meal of burger and chips or the odd bar of chocolate – it only becomes a problem if they are eating this way every day.

Before you begin to make changes to your child's diet, think carefully about what you hope to achieve. Be realistic, and aim for small changes rather than a total overhaul of your family's eating habits – and try not to nag your child to eat foods that they really don't like or insist they clear their plate if they are not hungry. Doing this will simply build up bad associations with healthy food and make your task significantly more difficult.

Aim for three meals and two healthy snacks each day and make lots of healthy foods available so that your child has the opportunity to discover what they like best. Just finding one vegetable and one fruit that your child enjoys can be enough to set them on the path to healthy eating, so don't put yourself under pressure to achieve too much too soon.

Did you know?
Evidence shows that children who don't eat breakfast tend to gain weight, so make time for your child to eat some cereal or toast even if you're running late.

A healthy diet

Our bodies require a variety of different foods to provide us with the energy and essential nutrients we need to stay fit and healthy. The food we eat can be split up into five different food groups, which form the building blocks of all our meals and snacks. These are as follows.

STARCHY FOODS SUCH AS BREAD, CEREALS, RICE, NOODLES AND PASTA

Guidelines suggest that the bulk of our diet should be made up of high-energy carbohydrate foods, so aim for four to six portions each day. These naturally low-fat foods contain fibre, B vitamins, vitamin E, essential fatty acids, and minerals including iron, zinc, magnesium and phosphorous. It's best to opt for wholegrain products, such as wholewheat and multigrain bread, wholewheat pasta, brown rice and porridge oats, instead of white bread, white rice and pasta, as these contain more fibre, which helps to prevent constipation. You should also avoid products which contain added fat and sugar, such as cakes, biscuits and sugary breakfast cereals, as these have more calories and can lead to weight gain.

VEGETABLES

Different vegetables contain energy-giving carbohydrates, vitamins and minerals, so aim to eat a wide variety. Fresh vegetables are best, but it's fine to choose frozen or canned, provided that they don't contain added salt or sugar. Many vegetables can be eaten raw, which is a great way to maximize their nutritional value – otherwise try to cook them lightly, and avoid adding butter or oil. Steaming, stir-frying, lightly boiling or baking, are all good ways to cook vegetables. If your child refuses to eat vegetables, disguise them by chopping them finely and mixing them into casseroles, pasta dishes and stews, or blending them into soups. Aim for three servings each day.

FRUITS

Like vegetables, fruits are also packed with vitamins, minerals and fibre, along with health-giving antioxidants and phytonutrients, so it's advisable to eat a wide variety of different types. Fresh fruit is the best option, but canned fruit is acceptable, provided it is packed in juice rather than syrup. Aim for two servings each day.

PROTEIN-RICH FOODS SUCH AS MEAT, POULTRY, FISH, EGGS, BEANS, LENTILS AND NUTS

Protein foods are essential for tissue growth and repair, and
children need between two and four portions daily. Red meat is
the richest source of protein and vitamin B12, which is essential
for the formation of red blood cells and the normal functioning of
the nervous system. However, meat can be high in fat, so it's best
to choose leaner cuts and trim off any visible fat before serving.
Poultry, pork and fish are also important sources of protein, and
oily fish is also rich in Omega-3 fats, which can reduce the risk of
heart disease and promote the development of healthy brain tissue
in babies and young children.

Vegetarians can meet their protein requirements by eating eggs,
beans, tofu, nuts and seeds. Legumes and pulses such as lentils and
chickpeas are particularly good as they are low in fat, and relatively
inexpensive. Peanut butter is another good option, although it is
high in fat, so shouldn't be consumed to excess. Whole nuts should
never be given to young children, because of the risk of choking.
Processed meats such as sausages and bacon, along with deli meats
such as ham, sliced chicken and turkey or pepperoni are not good
choices as they are high in fat and usually high in salt.

in a non-stick pan with a little olive oil, and serve them with oven-baked wedges, sweetcorn and tomato ketchup.

DAIRY PRODUCTS SUCH AS MILK, CHEESE, YOGHURT AND FROMAGE FRAIS

Dairy products such as milk and cheese contain calcium, which strengthens bones and teeth and helps nerves and muscles to work properly. They also contain protein, phosphorous, vitamins A and B and zinc. As dairy products contain high levels of saturated fat, reduced fat options should be introduced as children grow older. Until the age of two, children should be given full-fat dairy products, but between the ages of two and five, children can be offered semi-skimmed milk. After the age of five, children no longer need the extra fat in dairy products, so can be given skimmed milk and low-fat cheeses. Children can also get calcium from almonds, Brazil nuts, bread, chickpeas, dried fruit and sardines. Aim for between two and four portions of calcium-rich foods per day.

Five-a-day

We've all heard that we should be eating five portions of fruit and vegetables each day, and although that sounds like a lot, it's surprisingly easy to achieve. Offer a glass of juice with breakfast, pack a small banana and a few carrot sticks in your child's lunch box, and serve two vegetables with dinner – and you will easily meet the daily target. Just remember that potatoes don't count as one of your five a day, and only one fruit juice or smoothie counts towards your daily total.

PORTION SIZE

Once you understand which foods your child should be eating, it's important to think about portion size. It can be tricky to know exactly how much your child should be eating, as there are no official guidelines. But, obviously, young children do not need to eat as much as adults. Instead, you should provide small portions of food that contain lots of calories and nutrients.

For this reason, it's best to avoid giving under-fives too many high-fibre foods, as this can fill them up so much that they can't eat as much as they need to provide them with adequate calories. Like adults, older children will do best on a diet that is low in fat and high in fibre, but they will require larger portions, and by the time they reach their teens, most children's energy requirements will exceed their parents'. Until then, it's best to offer children half to two-thirds of an adult-sized portion, depending on their age and activity levels.

Did you know?
It takes 20 minutes for your brain to register that your stomach is full. This means that it's very easy to eat more than you need – so encourage your child to eat slowly and don't offer second helpings straight away.

Did you know?
If your child tries a new food and doesn't like it, it's worth trying again a few weeks later. It can take up to ten attempts before a child accepts a new food, so they may grow up to like cabbage after all!

Foods to restrict or avoid

Some foods have very little nutritional value, and should make up only a small part of your child's diet. These include cakes, biscuits, crisps, sweets, chocolate, fizzy drinks and fried foods. Of course, these foods tend to be very popular with children – and adults! – but it's very important to restrict the quantity that your child consumes.

Sugary foods are particularly popular with children, but they are best described as 'empty calories' – although they provide a brief surge of energy, they don't contain any nutrients at all. These foods can also be quite addictive as the energy they provide is almost immediate, but fades quickly and leaves us wanting more and more. As a result it's very easy to overeat sugary foods, which is why they are so clearly linked to weight gain – and they are bad for your child's teeth too.

High-fat foods such as chips, crisps and pastries are also bad news. Eating these foods regularly will almost certainly cause your child to gain weight. They can also raise blood cholesterol and lead to heart disease in later life, so try to limit the amount of fried foods that your child eats. If your child is fond of takeaways, then you may find that the best solution is to prepare their favourites at home, where you can choose to grill or bake instead of fry.

Arguably the worst foods of all are those that contain large amounts of fat and sugar. Cakes, biscuits and chocolate fall into this category, and they spell disaster for your child's health and wellbeing – not to mention their waistline. If you feel that your child eats too many of these foods, then your best tactic is to stop buying them. If these foods aren't kept in the house, then your child is more likely to accept a healthy alternative, and should eventually get out of the habit of eating these kind of snacks.

Bear in mind that it's not a good idea to ban these foods altogether, but it's best to restrict them to one or two servings per week. Many families find that it works well to restrict these kinds of foods to the weekend – but do keep an eye on portion size as your efforts will be for nothing if your child eats several bars of chocolate in one go! You may find that it helps to buy fun-size chocolate bars and small packets of crisps – and store them at the top of the cupboard where your child can't get at them. It's very easy to overeat this kind of food, so offering your child a full-size bar of chocolate or family-size packet of crisps will almost certainly encourage them to eat too much.

Is a bad diet linked to bad behaviour?
Nathan has always been a handful, but as he got older his temper tantrums seemed to get worse, instead of better. I didn't worry too much until he started school, but then

he started getting into fights with other children and his teachers said that he wasn't behaving himself in class and was falling behind.

We tried everything we could think of to encourage Nathan to behave, including banning television and computer games. One day we were called into school because he had sworn at a teacher. We were running out of punishments so we came up with the idea of banning sweets, crisps, biscuits, fizzy drinks and takeaways – all his favourite treats – for two weeks.

Nathan really wasn't happy about it, but after a while he realized that he would have to eat fruit or yoghurt if he was hungry instead of having biscuits or sweets. Instead of his usual chips he ate whatever we were eating – and because he hadn't filled himself up with junk food we were amazed when he ate everything we put in front of him.

After about ten days, we started to notice that Nathan's behaviour was improving. He was hardly having any temper tantrums, was going to bed without complaining and he seemed much calmer and happier. We wondered if cutting out the junk food made a difference, so we decided to carry on focusing on healthy foods.

Now Nathan only has sweets and chocolates once a week, he drinks juice instead of fizzy drinks and has burger and fries as an occasional treat. It could be a coincidence, but he's doing much better at school and is staying out of trouble. I only wish we'd thought about changing his diet sooner.

Leona is mum to Nathan, seven.

Fat facts

Most of us assume that fat is bad, but this is not strictly true. In fact babies and young children need a high-fat diet to help them grow and develop, and older children and adults need small amounts of fat to keep us healthy. Babies and young children usually get all the fats they need from breast milk and dairy products, while older children and adults can get more than enough from eating healthy foods that are naturally high in fat, such as milk, cheese and yoghurt, oily fish, nuts, seeds and avocados.

There are actually four main types of fat in our foods, and some of them are better for us than others. The following list will help you to identity which to include in your child's diet and which to avoid.

- ▶ *Saturated fat: These are usually solid at room temperature, and come mostly from animal sources such as butter, lard and suet. These fats can raise blood cholesterol, which clogs up the arteries and causes heart disease, so it's best to keep these fats to a minimum.*
- ▶ *Unsaturated fat: These are normally soft or liquid at room temperature and are usually of vegetable origin. Sources include oily fish, nuts and seeds, avocado and sunflower and olive oils. These fats should be used in place of saturated fats wherever possible.*
- ▶ *Essential fatty acids: Also known as Omega 3 and Omega 6, these are the healthiest of all fats and are found in oily fish and some vegetable oils, respectively. Omega-3 fats can protect against heart disease and cancer, so it's advisable to include them in your child's diet.*
- ▶ *Hydrogenated trans fats: These are the worst fats of all. They are produced in the food manufacturing process as a means to solidify vegetable oils. They are commonly found in margarine, ready meals, takeaways, cakes, biscuits, crisps and sauces. Like saturated fats, they can increase the risk of heart disease, so are best avoided.*

You should never consider restricting your child's fat intake until they are over the age of two because until this point they need to get almost half their daily calories from fat. Children over the age of two need about 30 per cent of their daily calories from fat, so if you think your child may be consuming more than this – and most children are – then there are a few simple steps you can take to reduce their intake.

▶ *Avoid fried food and try to grill or bake foods instead.*
▶ *Choose low-fat dairy products and semi-skimmed milk for children over the age of two.*
▶ *Use minimal amounts of butter, margarine and mayonnaise – and use low-fat alternatives where possible.*
▶ *Limit the amount of fast-food meals and snacks such as crisps, cakes and chocolate that your child eats, as these contain high levels of fat.*
▶ *Choose lean cuts of meat, trim off any excess fat and remove the skin from chicken after cooking.*

Learning to limit salt

Most of us eat too much salt, but it's very important to keep children's salt intake to a minimum. Consuming too much sodium, which is found in salt, can lead to health problems such as high blood pressure and heart disease in later life. Children who develop a taste for salty foods will find it harder to give them up as they get older, so it's best to restrict their consumption from the start.

The maximum amount of salt that children should consume depends on their age, although it's a good idea to eat less than this, if possible.

▶ *1–3 years: 2 g a day (0.8 g sodium)*
▶ *4–6 years: 3 g a day (1.2 g sodium)*
▶ *7–10 years: 5 g a day (2 g sodium)*
▶ *11 and over: 6 g a day (2.5 g sodium).*

Most of the salt we consume comes from eating processed foods, which are usually high in salt. Breakfast cereals, bread, biscuits, soups, sauces, ready meals and crisps all contain high levels of salt, and foods such as cheese, bacon, pickles, and smoked fish are also very salty.

To keep your child's salt consumption to a minimum, avoid adding salt when you are cooking or serving food, limit their consumption of salty snacks, and make sure that salty foods such as sausages, burgers and chicken nuggets are not a regular part of their diet.

If you are buying packaged food, then read the label before you buy to make sure that it isn't high in salt. If it is, then try to find a healthier alternative.

Insight

Just because you don't add salt to your child's food, don't assume that they are well within the recommended guidelines. Processed foods are the worst offenders – and many seemingly healthy foods such as bread and breakfast cereals can be surprisingly high in sodium. Check the packaging before you buy and make sure that high-salt foods don't feature in your child's daily diet.

Did you know?

Fizzy drinks and squashes contain more sugar that any other item in most children's diets.

Making sense of food labels

It's not always as easy as you might think to tell the difference between healthy and unhealthy foods. For example, many packaged foods contain hidden salt and sugar and food manufacturers often add extra sugar to 'healthy' low-fat foods to make them taste better. For this reason, always check the nutritional guidelines, which are printed on the labels of all packets, jars and cans of food.

Many supermarket brands now display a 'traffic light' or 'wheel' labelling system on the front of the packet to make it easier to understand the calorie, fat, sugar and salt content of foods. If the calorie, fat or sugar content is printed on a red

(Contd)

area, it indicates that the product contains a high level, amber shows medium and green shows low. Try to limit foods that show high levels and make fresh produce or packaged foods that are mostly 'green' or 'amber' the basis of your diet. It's also worth remembering that ingredients are always listed in descending order, with the main ingredient first, so avoid any products that list sugar (including sucrose, dextrose, glucose syrup or high fructose corn syrup) or fats in the top three ingredients.

Food manufacturers also use lots of little tricks to make foods seem healthier and more appealing than they really are. For example, just because a food is labelled 'no added sugar', it doesn't necessarily mean that it's sugar free, as it could have been sweetened with fruit juice instead. By the same token, words such as 'healthy', 'lite', 'fresh', 'natural' and 'farmhouse' are essentially meaningless. They are often used to make foods sound nutritious and appealing, but have no legal meaning and don't tell you anything at all about the quality or healthiness of the product inside.

Dealing with cravings

If your child seems to be hungry all the time, they are probably confusing cravings with a genuine need to eat. Constantly giving in to cravings is one of the easiest ways to gain weight, particularly as the foods that most children crave are high in sugar and fat. The trouble is, banning these foods completely is likely to make your child crave them even more, and increases the likelihood that your child will overindulge whenever they get the chance.

If your child has eaten a proper meal, they are unlikely to be hungry for three to four hours, so if they ask for more food before this time, they are probably craving food that they don't really need. Children are particularly vulnerable to cravings when:

- *they see sweets in a shop and don't want to go home without some*
- *they see foods advertised on television*
- *they see or smell foods when they pass a shop or takeaway*
- *they see a favourite food and want to taste it*
- *they are at the cinema, watching television or in any other situation where they would usually snack.*

Usually cravings pass within a few minutes, so you may find it helpful to ask your child to wait for ten minutes before you give in to their demands. By the time this time has passed you may find that they have forgotten or lost interest. Distraction also works well, so try to engage your child in other activities, such as playing a game, reading a book or going for a walk. If these techniques don't work, then your child may be genuinely hungry, so keep a supply of healthy snacks on hand to offer as an alternative.

Provided your child is eating a balanced diet, they shouldn't have too many cravings – but they will inevitably happen from time to time. However, this isn't necessarily a bad thing as it's a good idea to teach your child how to deal with cravings – and they won't learn this if you don't allow them to indulge every once in a while. Keep an eye on portion sizes so that they don't overeat, and try to offer healthier options, such as frozen yoghurt instead of ice cream. Remember, teaching your child to control their urges to eat unhealthy foods and to limit the amount they consume is a valuable lesson, and one that could help prevent them gaining weight in the future.

Insight

Banning unhealthy foods altogether often causes more problems further down the line. I've been to children's parties where the only food available is fruit and crudities, and although such dedication to healthy eating is very noble, given half a chance these same children have a tendency to gorge themselves on junk food until they are sick – which is usually at another child's party! It's far more helpful to teach

(Contd)

your child that there's no such thing as good or bad foods – provided that they are only eaten in moderation.

Family meals

In recent years it has become the norm for children to eat totally different foods to their parents – mostly because longer working hours has made it impossible for many families to eat together at a reasonable time. Unfortunately, what many of us regard as 'children's foods' aren't the healthiest options. Sausages, fish fingers, chicken nuggets, baked beans and burgers are all high in salt, and don't get children into the habit of eating different flavours and textures.

Your child is much more likely to experiment with different foods if they see you eating them too, so make the effort to eat together as a family as often as you can – even if it's only at weekends. Consider placing bowls of food in the centre of the table so that everyone can serve themselves, as this allows children to feel that they have some control over what they eat. They are more likely to eat foods that they have put on their own plate and you may find that they are more willing try new foods if they see other people tucking in.

Eating together at the table is a good way to spend time together as a family and catch up on the events of the day. It can also improve your child's table manners and encourage them to eat consciously and take their time over their food. We are more likely to overeat if we eat in front of the television, so make the effort to lay the table and sit down together without any distractions.

Most families can manage to eat together at least once a day – after all, it only takes five or ten minutes to sit down to a bowl of cereal or a slice of toast every morning for breakfast. But if it's not practical for you to do this, there are ways to make sure that your child still gets the benefit of family meals. Rather than relying on 'child friendly' foods from the freezer section of your supermarket, consider preparing the evening meal a little earlier, so that your child can eat first. Alternatively, you could save some leftovers from the night before and use them for your child's tea the following day. If neither of these options are workable, then think about batch cooking some family meals at the weekend and freezing them until you need them. Freeze individual portions for your child that can be defrosted and heated up quickly. This is just as convenient as relying on ready meals or conventional frozen food, but much more nutritious. Even if you only manage to do this twice a week, it's better than relying on convenience foods every day.

Case study: Dealing with a fussy eater

The problem

Zoe is a six-year-old girl who will only eat a very limited number of foods and who often eats the same things every day. She will only eat one type of breakfast cereal, cheese sandwiches on white bread, and sausages or fish fingers for dinner. She won't eat fruit and the only vegetable she will eat is peas. Her parents are worried that she isn't getting a balanced diet, but can't persuade her to try anything new.

The solution

Zoe's parents, Natasha and Ben, decided to get her involved in the foods she eats, so took her on a special trip to the supermarket to look for foods that she might enjoy. The only condition was that she had to choose one item from each section of the supermarket. They then arranged small amounts of each food on saucers and encouraged Zoe to try each one in turn, and reassured her that she

(Contd)

could spit it out if she didn't like it. Zoe didn't like everything she tried, but she found five new foods that she would eat: grapes, mini pitta bread, prawns, babycorn and pasta shells.

Zoe's parents noticed that she preferred small-sized, or individual foods so made an effort to create appealing mini meals.

The outcome

As a result of this new approach, Zoe started eating home-made mini meatballs in tomato sauce, home-made mini chicken burgers and even ate her own mini portion of shepherd's pie, which was served in its own ramekin.

After the first tasting experiment, Zoe's parents also encouraged her to taste whatever they were eating. As a result, Zoe discovered that she also likes new potatoes, tortelloni and green beans.

Although she made slow progress at first, Zoe is now eating a much wider range of foods, and will now eat the same, or similar, meals to her parents. By focusing on what she will eat, rather than what she won't, her parents have taken the tension out of mealtimes and helped Zoe to be more relaxed around food.

Eating out

Restaurant foods and takeaways shouldn't be a regular part of your child's diet, but there's no harm in indulging every once in a while. However, some options are better than others, so encourage your child to make the healthiest choices.

▶ *In burger restaurants, opt for regular rather than the super-size option. Avoid extras such as cheese, bacon and mayonnaise, and order small fries with water, fruit juice or a diet drink.*
▶ *When ordering pizza, order thin crust instead of deep pan, choose lots of vegetable toppings and avoid fatty meats such as pepperoni or ground beef. Some restaurants give you the option to choose reduced-fat cheese too.*

- Chinese food can be a great choice if you avoid deep fried dishes and heavy sauces. Look for stir-fried chicken, beef or seafood with vegetables and opt for steamed rice instead of fried.
- Indian food can be very high in calories, so avoid creamy curries and naan bread. Instead, order grilled meats or curries with a tomato sauce base, served with basmati rice and vegetables.
- Kebabs can be healthier than you think. Choose chicken instead of lamb or fatty donner meat, and stay clear of high-fat dressings such as mayonnaise. Serve with salad instead of chips, or split a portion between two.
- Pre-packed sandwiches can contain more calories than a burger and are often very high in fat and salt, so choose carefully. Avoid deep-filled sandwiches and look for chicken or fish with salad and minimal mayonnaise. A wrap is usually a better option.
- Chip shop food is notoriously fatty, so is really best avoided. Pies and battered sausages are particularly bad choices, so consider sharing a portion of fish and chips and serving with peas.

Packed lunches

School meals are much healthier than they were, but many parents feel that their child is better off with a packed lunch. Depending on the types of meals available at your school, this may be true. Many schools do now offer children a choice between healthy options and fried foods, but the fact remains that most children will still opt for chips and beans over a baked potato with salad unless there is someone on hand to ensure that they are eating a balanced meal.

Unfortunately, a badly planned packed lunch can be just as unhealthy – if not worse – than a typical school meal. A white bread ham sandwich with a packet of crisps, biscuit and fizzy drink does not constitute a healthy meal. Instead, you should make sure that all the major food groups are represented, so that your child has enough energy to get them through the school day without getting hungry and being tempted by sugary snacks.

Ideally, your child's packed lunch should contain:

▶ *one carbohydrate food, such as bread, pasta or rice*
▶ *one protein food, such as meat, chicken, fish or eggs*
▶ *one dairy food, such as cheese, milk or yoghurt*
▶ *one portion of vegetables, such as salad in a sandwich, cherry tomatoes or carrot sticks*
▶ *one portion of fruit.*

It's a good idea to plan what you will need for your child's lunchbox in advance, so that you are well prepared and they don't get stuck with the same foods every day, as this will get boring very quickly. Think about varying traditional sandwiches with rolls, wraps, pittas or bagels – or you could make up individual servings of rice, pasta or potato salad. Always add lettuce, tomato and cucumber to sandwiches, or add sweetcorn, chopped peppers and tomatoes to salads. Carrot sticks, slices of pepper and chunks of cucumber also work well with a hummus dip.

Cold meat or chicken or tinned tuna are ideal as sandwich fillings or salad ingredients, and mini cheeses or a hard-boiled egg are also a good way to add some protein. A carton of yoghurt or fromage frais, along with a portion of fruit makes a great pudding, and a frozen carton of fruit juice inside your child's lunchbox will keep everything cool until they are ready to eat.

Insight

Young children often have an aversion to sandwiches, especially if they go soggy. You might find they are happier with squares, triangles or fingers of bread, a slice of ham or turkey and some chopped cucumber and sweetcorn. You can wrap or pack each ingredient individually, so that your child can assemble their own sandwich or eat each ingredient separately.

Resist the urge to give your child an apple or banana every day, as they will soon get fed up with this and it may well end up in the bin. They are much more likely to enjoy fruit if you chop up grapes, cherries, pineapple, or whatever is in season, and serve it in a sealed pot. Save time by making a batch at the start of the week, and the whole family can enjoy it as a healthy dessert.

Should you go organic?

Organic farmers are governed by strict regulations, which restrict the use of artificial, chemical fertilizers and pesticides, and prevent the routine use of drugs, growth hormones and antibiotics when raising animals. More of us than ever before are prepared to pay extra for organic produce. But is it worth it?

Some people buy organic foods because they think that they taste better. Others buy them because they put a premium on animal welfare or because they worry about the environmental impact of conventional farming. It's certainly true that some organic foods contain higher levels of nutrients than non-organic alternatives. For example, organic milk is higher in Omega-3 fatty acids, vitamin E and vitamin A than non-organic milk and, on average, organic foods contain higher levels of vitamin C, calcium, magnesium, iron and chromium, as well as cancer-fighting antioxidants. Food experts believe that organic meat really is worth the extra money, simply because it's free from all the drugs that are administered to intensively reared animals.

Few of us can afford to buy only organic foods, but it's arguably worth spending the extra money on some foods, if you can. For example, when buying fruit and vegetables, it's not worth paying the extra for foods such as oranges and bananas, which have a thick skin to protect them from pesticides. You would do better to spend the extra money on vegetables such as broccoli and cauliflower, which are more exposed to pesticides used in conventional farming. However,

(Contd)

as a general rule of thumb, the more you eat of a particular food, the more it's probably worth buying organic if you can.

If buying organic food isn't an option, then peeling fruit and vegetables, and cutting the tops off root vegetables, removes the areas that may have been exposed to pesticides.

Grow your own

Children are often more willing to eat fruit and vegetables if they have helped to grow them. If you have a garden, then turn a small section into a vegetable patch and ask your child to help you tend it. Tomatoes, strawberries, lettuce, green beans, peas and carrots are popular choices, and some of them can be grown in pots and containers if you don't have much outdoor space.

TEST YOUR KNOWLEDGE

1 *How many snacks should your child have each day?*

2 *Can you name the five essential food groups?*

3 *At what age can you introduce semi-skimmed milk?*

4 *How many portions of fruit and vegetables should your child consume each day?*

5 *How many portions of starchy foods should your child consume each day?*

6 *How many portions of protein should your child consume each day?*

7 *Roughly what proportion of an adult portion should you offer to your child?*

8 *How many attempts can it take before a child starts to eat a new food?*

9 *What percentage of your child's diet should come from fat?*

10 *How much fluid should your child consume each day?*

....

Answers

1 *Two*

2 *Starches, vegetables, fruits, proteins, dairy*

3 *Two*

4 *Five*

5 *Four to six*

6 *Two to four*

7 *Two-thirds*

8 *Ten*

9 *Almost 50 per cent until the age of two, then 30 per cent*

10 *Six cups*

12

....

Fit for life

In this chapter you will learn:
- *how to make fitness a way of life*
- *how to deal with changing circumstances*
- *how to avoid slipping back into bad habits.*

Now that you have put so much time and effort into helping your child to get fit, it's important not to slip back into bad habits. As you have discovered, making a series of small changes really can get your family on track for a healthy future – and by now these changes are probably so much a part of your daily routine that they have become second nature.

Hopefully, you will have managed to find activities that your child enjoys so much that they need no persuasion to take part. However, it's true that a small minority of children will never be truly enthusiastic about sports and physical activities, so you may need to continue to cajole them to stay active. If this is the case, then don't be disheartened. Focus on maintaining an active lifestyle and encourage your child to try as many activities as possible. Eventually they should manage to find something that they can enjoy – so stay positive and remind yourself of everything you have achieved. Slow but steady progress is usually much easier to sustain – and as you're hoping to form habits that will last a lifetime there's really no need to make dramatic changes overnight.

As time goes on you will inevitably find that changing circumstances sometimes make it more difficult for you and your family to find the time to eat well and stay active. If this happens to you, resist the urge to adopt an all-or-nothing approach. Sticking rigidly to your routine will make life very difficult and stressful – and, as a result, you may decide that it's not worth the bother to cook a meal from scratch and take regular exercise when you could just sit down in front of the television with a takeaway. In order to stay fit and active for life, you will need to learn how to adapt to these changes while keeping your family's fitness high on your list of priorities. The following section covers some of the most common 'danger points' you are likely to encounter, and gives you tips on how to negotiate them.

Insight

Don't put yourself under too much pressure to eat healthily and exercise day in day out. As long as you observe the 80/20 rule – eat well and exercise for 80 per cent of the time – it doesn't matter if you allow your family the occasional treat or lazy weekend every once in a while.

Dealing with danger points

Have you embarked on a diet or fitness regime in the past, only to give it up and return to your old habits as soon as the novelty wears off? If so, you may well be worried and may be questioning whether you can keep up your efforts to help your child to get fit. However, if you have followed the advice and suggestions in this book, you should find that your new lifestyle isn't too difficult to sustain.

Fad diets and intense exercise regimes usually fail because they are so demanding and are at odds with your normal lifestyle. Sooner or later, real life gets in the way, you lose interest and you go in search of a new fad that will be easier or more effective – and so the cycle goes on. As you now know, there is no quick fix and you won't get results without putting in some effort. But hopefully, by finding sports and activities that fit with your family's lifestyle and eating a balanced diet that gives you all the energy you need to stay active, you won't be tempted to throw in the towel.

Insight

Keeping fit and active does take effort, and sometimes you will be tempted to give it up, eat what you like and relax on the sofa. If you can feel your reserve starting to slip, remind yourself of everything that you have achieved and how much better you and your family look and feel as a result. Focus on your achievements and think about your healthy future together and you should feel your motivation beginning to return.

You are very likely to encounter some, if not all, of the following scenarios at some point in the coming months or years, but if you follow the advice below you will be less likely to slip back into old habits and discover that it really is possible to stay fit for life.

BAD WEATHER

Many parents decide to introduce their child to sports and activities during the summer holidays. After all, this is when children have a significant amount of spare time to fill, and the warmer weather and longer daylight hours give plenty of opportunities for getting out in the fresh air. As a result, many families hit the first stumbling block when autumn arrives and the days get colder and darker.

If you suspect this will be an issue for your family, then plan some new activities well in advance. If your child enjoys indoor sports and activities, then they are unlikely to be affected, but it's a good idea to come up with some alternatives for children who like to play outdoors. Swimming is a great activity no matter what the weather – or you could turn the colder weather to your advantage and try out the outdoor skating rinks that open up in the winter.

Trips to the park and playground can continue no matter what the weather. Younger children always enjoy running through the autumn leaves or crunching through frosty grass – and if you invest in a pair of wellies, a raincoat and their own umbrella, they will be keen to get outside even when it's raining. To maintain your own fitness levels, try not to let the changing weather force you back into your car. If you have been walking your child to school or going to the shop on foot, then continue as normal if you possibly can.

Insight

Many children enjoy going outside in wet weather, and you'll have no excuse to stay indoors if you go shopping for some suitable wet weather clothes. Look for lightweight raincoats, wellies, rain hats and umbrellas – your child is less likely to complain about walking to school in the rain if they've got special clothes to keep them warm and dry.

TROUBLESOME TEENAGERS

Parents often struggle to motivate their teenagers to keep fit and eat healthily. This is the age when children are most likely to lose interest in sports, as their time and attention is taken up with other things. If this happens to your child, resist the urge to nag and try to understand that today's teenagers have a lot on their plate. It can be a struggle to keep up with their homework, prepare for exams and spend time with their friends and family, so sports or leisure activities are often the first things to slide.

At this stage, you may have to rethink the activities that you enjoy together as a family. Many teenagers will lose interest in team sports as they won't have the time for regular practice sessions, but you may find that offering to pay for a gym membership, buying some home exercise equipment or a fitness DVD will be all that's needed to keep them fit.

Teenagers are particularly image conscious, and girls in particular have a tendency to try out weight-loss diets and exercise regimes.

So remind your teen that eating sensibly and taking regular exercise will keep them in great shape, improve their energy levels and help to relieve exam stress. As you have already laid the foundations of a healthily lifestyle, this will hopefully be enough to stop them slipping into bad habits.

TAKING A BREAK

Most families find that they are more active than usual when they are on holiday. Even the most relaxing beach holiday usually involves daily swimming sessions and walks in the sunshine, but it also involves plenty of delicious, not to mention high-calorie foods. No one is suggesting that you should forgo holiday ice creams or eat salad for every meal, but it would be a shame to jeopardize all your hard work for the sake of a one- or two-week blowout.

Most of us will indulge in high-calorie foods at certain times of the year, such as Christmas, Easter and summer holidays, and there's nothing at all wrong with that – provided you get back to eating healthily afterwards. For this reason, it's not a good idea to allow your child to eat unlimited quantities of junk food just because it's a special occasion – only to tell them that they can't have it the next day. All parents know that it's important to be consistent, and throwing all your good intentions out of the window on high days and holidays sends a very confusing message.

If you are going to eat out or enjoy cakes, chocolate or ice cream, make it clear to your child that it's a special treat, and not something to be enjoyed every day. Try to follow your usual routine as much as possible – for example, make sure that everyone snacks on fruit and has salad or vegetables with every meal – and limit the amount of snack foods you buy, even on special occasions such as Christmas. If they are in the house, they will get eaten – so it's best not to buy too much to begin with.

Whether you're going away on holiday or having a few days off at home, there's absolutely nothing wrong with taking a break from your usual sport or leisure activities from time to time – after all, only the most dedicated among us are keen to exercise at Christmas or on our birthday. But don't leave it too long before you get back into your normal routine as the longer you put it off, the more likely you are to give it up altogether.

Insight

Setting new goals for yourself and your family will help you to stay motivated. Signing up for a fun run is a great way to keep adults and older children interested, while younger children will respond well to winning awards or moving up to a more advanced class.

ILLNESS OR INJURY

It's not advisable to exercise if you or your child is feeling unwell. This puts the body under unnecessary strain and can increase the risk of injury and dehydration. The same applies if you or your child has suffered an injury. The body needs time to recover, so take it easy until your doctor declares you fit and well.

It can be tough to get back into the habit of taking regular exercise if you have been unwell. Some childhood illnesses, such as chickenpox, can leave your child feeling under the weather for a few weeks and it can take time to get your strength back after a nasty bout of flu.

For this reason, build up slowly and don't jump straight back in where you left off. You may even find that a gentle form of exercise, such as swimming or walking, is a good way to keep the family active until you are able to resume your normal activities.

If your child attends sports clubs or classes, then you may find it helpful to get to know other parents so that you can drive each other's children to practice if one of you is out of action. Other parents can be a godsend on days when you're ill in bed, as they are usually only too happy to help out and organize a last-minute play date so that your child can get some exercise while you get some much-needed rest.

A final word

You are now armed with all the information that you need to help your child get fit and active. You have learned how to make small but important changes to your lifestyle, discovered ways that you can keep fit as a family and found out about a range of different sports and activities that are available to your child. If your child is overweight, you now have all the information you need to help them achieve and maintain a healthy weight, and you have also discovered how the foods we eat can help to improve your family's health and vitality.

Don't underestimate all you have achieved, because you have taken several important steps towards getting your child fit for life. So good luck to you and your family for a happy and healthy future – and well done!

10 THINGS TO REMEMBER

1 *Some children will always need extra encouragement to stay active, so be prepared to motivate your child to keep going.*

2 *Don't expect your family's habits to change overnight, but take stock of what you have achieved on a regular basis.*

3 *Don't be tempted by fad diets or radical training programmes – slow and steady progress is more likely to give lasting results.*

4 *Plan wet weather or winter activities well in advance. Bad weather isn't an excuse to give up exercise and watch television instead!*

5 *Teenagers often lose interest in exercise and activities, so think about paying for them to join a gym or exercise class, or buy a Wii Fit so that they can exercise with their friends.*

6 *Consistency is important – so save unhealthy foods for treats, and then only offer them in moderation.*

7 *Don't stock up on biscuits, cakes or crisps before birthdays or Christmas. Buy what you need and no more – anything extra will get eaten!*

8 *Stick to a routine of three healthy meals and two snacks and you and your family will be too full to eat unhealthy snacks.*

9 *Take it easy for a week or two following illness or injury.*

10 *Give yourself a pat on the back for your efforts – you have set your child on the path to be fit for life.*

Appendix I

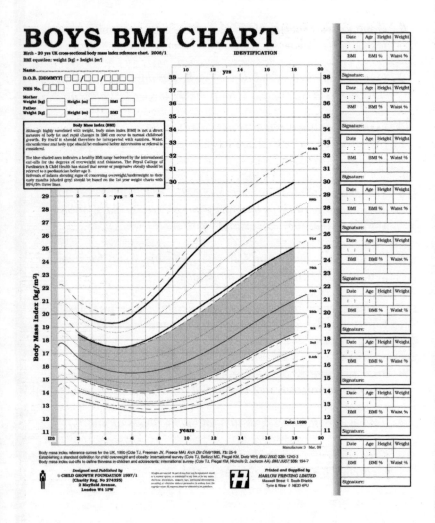

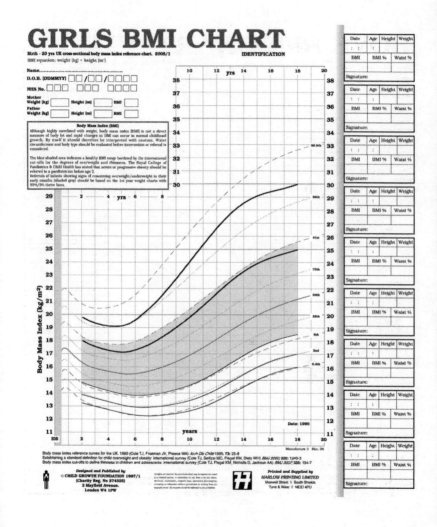

GIRLS BMI CHART

Birth - 20 yrs UK cross-sectional body mass index reference chart. 2008/1

BMI equation: weight [kg] ÷ height [m²]

IDENTIFICATION

Name.....................

D.O.B. [DDMMYY]

NHS No.

Mother
Weight [kg] Height [m] BMI

Father
Weight [kg] Height [m] BMI

Body Mass Index (BMI)

Although highly correlated with weight, body mass index [BMI] is not a direct measure of body fat and rapid changes in BMI can occur in normal childhood growth. By itself it should therefore be interpreted with caution. Waist circumference and body type should be evaluated before intervention or referral is considered.

The blue shaded area indicates a healthy BMI range bordered by the international cut-offs for the degrees of overweight and thinness. The Royal College of Paediatrics & Child Health has stated that severe or progressive obesity should be referred to a paediatrician before age 2.
Referrals of infants showing signs of concerning overweight/underweight in their early months [shaded grey] should be based on the 1st year weight charts with 99%/3% three lines.

Body mass index reference curves for the UK. 1990 (Cole TJ, Freeman JV, Preece MA) *Arch Dis Child* 1995; 73: 25-9
Establishing a standard definition for child overweight and obesity: international survey (Cole TJ, Bellizzi MC, Flegal KM, Dietz WH) *BMJ* 2000; 320: 1240-3
Body mass index cut-offs to define thinness in children and adolescents: international survey (Cole TJ, Flegal KM, Nicholls D, Jackson AA) *BMJ* 2007; 335: 194-7

Designed and Published by
◇ CHILD GROWTH FOUNDATION 1997/1
(Charity Reg. No 274325)
2 Mayfield Avenue,
London W4 1PW

Printed and Supplied by
HARLOW PRINTING LIMITED
Maxwell Street ◇ South Shields
Tyne & Wear ◇ NE33 4PU

Date	Age	Height	Weight
: :	:		
BMI	BMI %	Waist %	
Signature:			

Date	Age	Height	Weight
: :	:		
BMI	BMI %	Waist %	
Signature:			

Date	Age	Height	Weight
: :	:		
BMI	BMI %	Waist %	
Signature:			

Date	Age	Height	Weight
: :	:		
BMI	BMI %	Waist %	
Signature:			

Date	Age	Height	Weight
: :	:		
BMI	BMI %	Waist %	
Signature:			

Date	Age	Height	Weight
: :	:		
BMI	BMI %	Waist %	
Signature:			

Date	Age	Height	Weight
: :	:		
BMI	BMI %	Waist %	
Signature:			

Date	Age	Height	Weight
: :	:		
BMI	BMI %	Waist %	
Signature:			

Appendix II

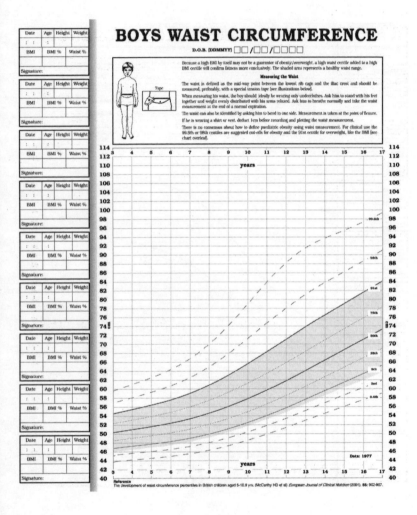

BOYS WAIST CIRCUMFERENCE

D.O.B. [DDMMYY] ☐☐ / ☐☐ / ☐☐☐☐

Because a high BMI by itself may not be a guarantee of obesity/overweight, a high waist centile added to a high BMI centile will confirm fatness more conclusively. The shaded area represents a healthy waist range.

Measuring the Waist

The waist is defined as the mid-way point between the lowest rib cage and the iliac crest and should be measured, preferably, with a special tension tape (see illustrations below).

When measuring his waist, the boy should ideally be wearing only underclothes. Ask him to stand with his feet together and weight evenly distributed with his arms relaxed. Ask him to breathe normally and take the waist measurement at the end of a normal expiration.

The waist can also be identified by asking him to bend to one side. Measurement is taken at the point of flexure.

If he is wearing a shirt or vest, deduct 1cm before recording and plotting the waist measurement.

There is no consensus about how to define paediatric obesity using waist measurement. For clinical use the 99.6th or 98th centiles are suggested cut-offs for obesity and the 91st centile for overweight, like the BMI (see chart overleaf).

Data: 1977

Reference
The development of waist circumference percentiles in British children aged 5-16.9 yrs. (McCarthy HD et al) *European Journal of Clinical Nutrition* (2001). **55:** 902-907.

GIRLS WAIST CIRCUMFERENCE

D.O.B. [DDMMYY] □□ /□□ /□□□□

Tape

Because a high BMI by itself may not be a guarantor of obesity/overweight, a high waist centile added to a high BMI centile will confirm fatness more conclusively. The shaded area represents a healthy waist range.

Measuring the Waist

The waist is defined as the mid-way point between the lowest rib cage and the iliac crest and should be measured, preferably, with a special tension tape [see illustrations below].

When measuring her waist, the girl should ideally be wearing only underclothes. Ask her to stand with her feet together and weight evenly distributed with her arms relaxed. Ask her to breathe normally and take the waist measurement at the end of a normal expiration.

The waist can also be identified by asking her to bend to one side. Measurement is taken at the point of flexure. If she is wearing a shirt or vest, deduct 1cm before recording and plotting the waist measurement.

There is no consensus about how to define paediatric obesity using waist measurement. For clinical use the 99.6th or 98th centiles are suggested cut-offs for obesity and the 91st centile for overweight, like the BMI [see chart overleaf].

Date	Age	Height	Weight
: :	:		
BMI	BMI %		Waist %
Signature:			

Date	Age	Height	Weight
: :	:		
BMI	BMI %		Waist %
Signature:			

Date	Age	Height	Weight
: :	:		
BMI	BMI %		Waist %
Signature:			

Date	Age	Height	Weight
: :	:		
BMI	BMI %		Waist %
Signature:			

Date	Age	Height	Weight
: :	:		
BMI	BMI %		Waist %
Signature:			

Date	Age	Height	Weight
: :	:		
BMI	BMI %		Waist %
Signature:			

Date	Age	Height	Weight
: :	:		
BMI	BMI %		Waist %
Signature:			

years

cm

99.6th
98th
91st
75th
50th
25th
9th
2nd
0.4th

Data: 1977

Reference
The development of waist circumference percentiles in British children aged 5-16.9 yrs: (McCarthy HD et al) *European Journal of Clinical Nutrition* (2001) 55: 902-907.

Taking it further

If you would like to know more about any of the sports, activities, issues or organizations mentioned in this book, the following contacts should be able to help you:

Sports and activities

(listed alphabetically by sport)
British Aikido Association www.aikido-baa.org.uk
American Football www.nfl.com
American Football (UK) www.bafa.org.uk
Grand National Archery Society www.archerygb.org
England Athletics www.englandathletics.org
Badminton England www.badmintonengland.co.uk
England Basketball www.englandbasketball.com
Bikeability www.bikeability.org.uk
British Canoe Union www.bcu.org.uk
The England And Wales Cricket Board
www.ecb.co.uk/development/kids/
British Cycling www.britishcycling.org.uk
National Dance Association www.aahperd.org/NDA/
British Fencing www.britishfencing.com
The Football Association www.thefa.com
Girlguiding UK www.girlguiding.org.uk
Children In Golf www.childreningolf.org
Gymboree www.gymboree-uk.com
British Gymnastics www.british-gymnastics.org/
England Hockey www.englandhockey.co.uk
British Horse Society www.bhs.org.uk
National Ice Skating Association www.iceskating.org.uk
British Judo www.britishjudo.org.uk
British Ju-Jitsu Association www.bjjagb.com

British Karate Association www.thebka.co.uk
National Karting Association www.nationalkarting.co.uk
British Kung Fu Association www.laugar-kungfu.com
Motor Sports Association www.msauk.org/
England Netball www.englandnetball.co.uk
The British Orienteering Federation www.britishorienteering.org.uk/
PADI www.padi.com
Rounders England www.roundersengland.co.uk
British Amateur Rugby League Association www.barla.org.uk
Rugby Football Union www.rfu.com
The Scout Association www.scouts.org.uk
United Kingdom Skateboarding Association www.ukskate.org.uk
British Surfing Association www.britsurf.co.uk
British Swimming www.swimming.org/britishswimming
Tae Kwon Do Association of Great Britain www.tagb.biz/
Tag Rugby UK www.tagrugby.co.uk/
Lawn Tennis Association www.lta.org.uk
Tumbletots www.tumbletots.com
Royal Yachting Association www.rya.org.uk

Useful contacts

Action for Blind People www.actionforblindpeople.org.uk
Action for Healthy Kids www.actionforhealthykids.org
Association for Physical Education www.afpe.org.uk
Asthma UK www.asthma.org.uk
The British Dietetic Association www.bdaweightwise.com
The British Heart Foundation www.bhf.org.uk/
Bullying UK www.bullying.co.uk
Butlins www.butlins.com
Carnegie Weight Management
www.carneigeweightmanagement.com
Center Parcs www.centerparcs.co.uk
Club la Manga www.lamangadirect.co.uk
Club la Santa www.clublasanta.co.uk
The Bobby Charlton Soccer School www.bcssa.co.uk

Diabetes UK www.diabetes.org.uk/
Harlow Healthcare www.healthforallchildren.co.uk
English Federation of Disability Sport www.efds.co.uk
The Food Standards Agency www.eatwell.gov.uk
Kidscape www.kidscape.org.uk
Little League www.littleleague.org
Mark Warner Holidays www.markwarner.co.uk
Mencap www.mencap.org.uk
The National Association for Sport and Physical Education
www.aahperd.org/naspe
The National Curriculum http://curriculum.qca.org.uk/
Obesity in America www.obesityinamerica.org
Parentline Plus www.parentlineplus.org.uk
PE4Life www.pe4life.org
PGL Holidays www.pgl.co.uk
Plas Menai www.plasmenai.co.uk
Pontins www.pontins.com
School Wellness Policies www.schoolwellnesspolicies.org
Ski Esprit www.esprit-holidays.co.uk
Ski Famille www.skifamille.co.uk
Sport England www.sportengland.org.uk
Sport Scotland www.sportscotland.org.uk
Sports Council for Wales www.sports-council-wales.org.uk
Sports Coach UK www.sportscoachuk.org
Weight Concern www.weightconcern.org.uk
Youth Sport Trust www.youthsporttrust.org

Index

Image credits